GUO FEIXIONG AND FREEDOM OF EXPRESSION IN CHINA

HEARING

BEFORE THE

SUBCOMMITTEE ON AFRICA, GLOBAL HEALTH, GLOBAL HUMAN RIGHTS, AND INTERNATIONAL ORGANIZATIONS

OF THE

COMMITTEE ON FOREIGN AFFAIRS HOUSE OF REPRESENTATIVES

ONE HUNDRED THIRTEENTH CONGRESS

FIRST SESSION

OCTOBER 29, 2013

Serial No. 113–102

Printed for the use of the Committee on Foreign Affairs

Available via the World Wide Web: http://www.foreignaffairs.house.gov/ or http://www.gpo.gov/fdsys/

U.S. GOVERNMENT PRINTING OFFICE

85–314PDF   WASHINGTON : 2013

For sale by the Superintendent of Documents, U.S. Government Printing Office
Internet: bookstore.gpo.gov   Phone: toll free (866) 512–1800; DC area (202) 512–1800
Fax: (202) 512–2104   Mail: Stop IDCC, Washington, DC 20402–0001

COMMITTEE ON FOREIGN AFFAIRS

EDWARD R. ROYCE, California, *Chairman*

CHRISTOPHER H. SMITH, New Jersey
ILEANA ROS-LEHTINEN, Florida
DANA ROHRABACHER, California
STEVE CHABOT, Ohio
JOE WILSON, South Carolina
MICHAEL T. McCAUL, Texas
TED POE, Texas
MATT SALMON, Arizona
TOM MARINO, Pennsylvania
JEFF DUNCAN, South Carolina
ADAM KINZINGER, Illinois
MO BROOKS, Alabama
TOM COTTON, Arkansas
PAUL COOK, California
GEORGE HOLDING, North Carolina
RANDY K. WEBER SR., Texas
SCOTT PERRY, Pennsylvania
STEVE STOCKMAN, Texas
RON DeSANTIS, Florida
TREY RADEL, Florida
DOUG COLLINS, Georgia
MARK MEADOWS, North Carolina
TED S. YOHO, Florida
LUKE MESSER, Indiana

ELIOT L. ENGEL, New York
ENI F.H. FALEOMAVAEGA, American
   Samoa
BRAD SHERMAN, California
GREGORY W. MEEKS, New York
ALBIO SIRES, New Jersey
GERALD E. CONNOLLY, Virginia
THEODORE E. DEUTCH, Florida
BRIAN HIGGINS, New York
KAREN BASS, California
WILLIAM KEATING, Massachusetts
DAVID CICILLINE, Rhode Island
ALAN GRAYSON, Florida
JUAN VARGAS, California
BRADLEY S. SCHNEIDER, Illinois
JOSEPH P. KENNEDY III, Massachusetts
AMI BERA, California
ALAN S. LOWENTHAL, California
GRACE MENG, New York
LOIS FRANKEL, Florida
TULSI GABBARD, Hawaii
JOAQUIN CASTRO, Texas

AMY PORTER, *Chief of Staff*   THOMAS SHEEHY, *Staff Director*
JASON STEINBAUM, *Democratic Staff Director*

———

SUBCOMMITTEE ON AFRICA, GLOBAL HEALTH, GLOBAL HUMAN RIGHTS, AND INTERNATIONAL ORGANIZATIONS

CHRISTOPHER H. SMITH, New Jersey, *Chairman*

TOM MARINO, Pennsylvania
RANDY K. WEBER SR., Texas
STEVE STOCKMAN, Texas
MARK MEADOWS, North Carolina

KAREN BASS, California
DAVID CICILLINE, Rhode Island
AMI BERA, California

CONTENTS

GUO FEIXIONG AND FREEDOM OF EXPRESSION IN CHINA

TUESDAY, OCTOBER 29, 2013

House of Representatives,
Subcommittee on Africa, Global Health,
Global Human Rights, and International Organizations,
Committee on Foreign Affairs,
Washington, DC.

The subcommittee met, pursuant to notice, at 2:30 p.m., Room 2255, Rayburn Building, Christopher Smith (chairman of the subcommittee) presiding.

Mr. SMITH. Let me begin by expressing my apologies for the delay. We had a series of votes before the House. Thank you for being here and thank you to our very distinguished witnesses on behalf of Mr. Stockman and I and other members of the subcommittee. Thank you for your extraordinary sacrifice that you bear on behalf of human rights. We so deeply appreciate it and respect it.

Today's hearing will focus on China's detention of writer, activist, and self-trained legal advocate Guo Feixiong. A veteran of China's rights defense movement, Mr. Guo was criminally detained on August 8, 2013 which I would note parenthetically, it is Baba, or Chinese Father's Day. I know Ms. Yang would love to be with her father and yet on that very day he was taken away by the security apparatus of the Chinese Government. We know that he wasn't formally arrested until early September 2013. Mr. Guo's detention appears to be a reprisal for his support of government transparency and calls for accountability. In recent months, Beijing has cracked down harshly on dozens of similarly minded advocates seeking political reforms.

Mr. Guo is not a newcomer to public advocacy nor to suffering, punishments and sacrifice for his work. A former novelist and businessman, he first became widely known in 2005 for organizing protests of land seizures on the outskirts of Guangzhou. In 2007, a Chinese court sentenced the outspoken Mr. Guo to 5 years' imprisonment on charges of illegal publishing. He and his supporters maintain the charges were fabricated to silence him and to silence the others. In late 2011, he was released. Since that time, he has continued to participate in China's rights defense movement. He has continued to express himself freely in the hopes of advancing human rights. He has protested along reporters fighting the Southern Weekly's heavy-handed censorship and vocally supported recent calls for greater government transparency and an end to corruption.

Now, Mr. Guo is being held on charges of ''assembling a crowd to disrupt order in a public place.'' This alleged crime, along with many others, is all too often employed unjustly against the courageous men and women who want accountability or are pressing for change. For simply asking for transparency, he is suspected of disrupting the harsh order that Beijing enforces. Notwithstanding China's own criminal procedure rules, authorities have denied Mr. Guo access to a lawyer and have failed to properly notify his family. Once again, China continues to enforce its legal protections haphazardly, if at all, when punishing or silencing those who advocate for reform and change.

Today's hearing is on the heroism and the sacrifices of Mr. Guo—that's what we are focusing on; this brave man needs to be lifted up. The United States Congress is focusing and expressing its profound respect as well as for his family. Sadly, Mr. Guo is one among many who are suffering in China today. In recent months. Chinese authorities have cracked down on dozens of human rights advocates participating in a so-called New Citizens' Movement. The movement, which began forming last year, has been described as a loose network of like-minded academics and lawyers who hold informal gatherings and promote various issues, including transparency and anti-corruption efforts.

These detentions signify Chinese citizens' growing resolve and Beijing's growing fears. Mr. Guo, and many others throughout China, want and deserve change. They want accountability, they want transparency, and they want basic human rights and respect for those rights and they want justice. And, increasingly, they are willing to endure even greater risks and willing to sacrifice their own personal security to speak freely.

We are fortunate today to be joined by Ms. Zhang Qing, Mr. Guo's courageous wife, and Ms. Yang Tianjiao, his wonderful daughter. We look forward to their testimony, their insights, and their defense of a beloved husband and father. We are also blessed to have with us two giants in the human rights field, Pastor Bob Fu and Mr. Chen Guangcheng, who will be speaking to us via Skype. He was supposed to be here personally, but was not feeling well enough to be here. We are also joined by Mr. Kumar, himself a political prisoner who suffered for his beliefs so many years ago and has been a frequent, very significant contributor to our efforts on the committee and for the Congress itself.

With this current crackdown on Chinese human rights activists, it is important to understand the brave and bold people challenging the Chinese state. And they are doing it in a nonviolent and in a benign way, and yet they are harshly retaliated against. Inspiring figures like Mr. Guo put another heroic face on these detentions. His face, however, does more than just contextualize the current crackdown or add details to a prisoner file. It causes us to wonder about ourselves, about our commitment to human rights, and the risks we are willing to take for those around us and in persecuted countries like the People's Republic of China. Mr. Guo now faces an uncertain punishment, and we must determine our own human rights commitment to him and others.

In July 2013, Mr. Guo wrote about a 1989 Tiananmen activist now facing the possibility of more prison time. He wrote that ''Zhao Changqing is an important symbol of the 1989 generation, who, in the face of danger, takes action, bears responsibility, persists, pushes forward, and becomes more involved. This is how one should behave and shoulder his fate.''

Despite the hardships and the odds, Mr. Guo reminds us that we, Members of Congress living in the safe harbors of the West, must shoulder our responsibilities and our burdens. Far too often, we don't. We are here today to accept our responsibility to Mr. Guo and other courageous Chinese human rights advocates. We hope that we also in his words will ''take action, bear responsibility, persist, push forward, and evolve'' like these heroes. He reminds us that this is how we all should behave.

We hope that the Chinese Government is listening. We hope the Chinese citizens seeking change are listening. And we hope Mr. Guo is listening. We hope President Obama and our administration are listening as well and will everything in their power to help free Mr. Guo and others fighting for human rights. We hope the U.S. Congress is listening, so that he will be freed and be out of that terrible, terrible gulag state.

I would now like to go to Mr. Stockman for any opening comments you may have.

Mr. STOCKMAN. I want to thank the chairman for putting this together and as I said to the television cameras, the Chinese Government would have greater respect from the people if they respected the people. And the fact that they are continually suppressing their own people—severely, according to independent reports—and are increasing the persecution of their own citizens. This is the wrong direction to go.

I think that prior to the Olympics, they were trying to be more open and more receiving of people's inputs. But since the Olympics, it seems like there is an increase of persecution in China and we, as congressmen, need to speak out and support those that are being persecuted. I thank the chairman again for offering this hearing for us to put a highlight on exactly what is going on in China.

Mr. SMITH. Mr. Stockman, thank you very much. Mr. Meadows.

Mr. MEADOWS. Thank you, Mr. Chairman, it is good to have you here, good to see many of you again. And as we look at this particular case, highlighting this case, I think what the American people need to hear, and quite frankly, what the world needs to hear is the injustice that we see, not only in the case of Mr. Guo, but really in terms of human rights in general in China.

I was part of a briefing just the other day as we started to look at the freedom of expression and how the story is not getting told and it is being subtly and at times not so subtly hidden from the citizens of China and from the rest of the world. According to World Press Freedom Index, China ranks 173rd about of 179 countries in terms of free press. That is a statistic that is unacceptable for a world leader and for a member of the U.N. Security Council.

And as we see the great reforms that have been promised as part of the 2012 elections, yet we hear today and we will hear today how those reforms have yet to take place. And so while these matters may be inherently an internal issue for China, as members of the United States Congress, it is our duty to expose the challenges that the Chinese citizens face and urge the government to implement the necessary reforms.

I want to thank the chairman for his unrelenting effort on behalf of people that perhaps have no voice other than his to stand up for human rights and I am proud to join him arm in arm to fight that battle. And with that, I yield back, Mr. Chairman.

Mr. SMITH. Mr. Meadows, thank you very much. We are joined by a member of the Congressional-Executive Commission on China and distinguished member of the House of Representatives, Mr. Pittenger, who is here because of his deep concern for human rights in China, as well as the rest of the world, and religious freedom in particular.

Mr. Pittenger.

Mr. PITTENGER. Thank you, Mr. Chairman, and thank you for your dedication as I have observed you the last 30 years. You have been a remarkable leader for the cause of human rights and religious liberties.

We gave up a lot in the late 1990s when we gave up Most Favored Nation trading status and we no longer have leverage on human rights and religious liberties. I regret we did that. There was a lot of business pressure and response to that. But nonetheless, you all have fought a valiant war. I have been over there a number of times and I am back there in January. We will do everything to support your efforts of very dedicated people who want to present the gospel in a fearless way. So God bless you for your service. I know that there are many here who pray for you and support you in your work. And only eternity will know the life that you have lived and what you have fought for and what you commit yourself to. Thank you.

Mr. SMITH. Mr. Pittenger, thank you so very much for you eloquence and to all of my colleagues for their steadfast support for fundamental human rights and for being so consistent. It is just so admirable and so encouraging.

I would like now to introduce our distinguished witnesses beginning first with the wife of Mr. Guo, Zhang Qing. She is a political asylee from China. In 2006, after her husband was arrested and badly tortured, she wrote open letters to the President of China and to President Bush to expose the brutality and torture that was happening to her husband. She also called for human rights organizations and the media to recognize and consider Chen Guangcheng's case while he was in jail. She and her husband's activities caused her to endure sustained pressure so she came to the United States. She now lives in Mr. Stockman's state, the great State of Texas and is a full-time university student there. And thank you for being here. I look forward, along with my colleagues, to your testimony.

We will then hear from Ms. Yang Tianjiao who is the daughter of Guo Feixiong. She came to the U.S. 4 years ago and is now a high school student in Texas where she won the President's Education Award for outstanding academic excellence in 2010. She loves music and art. She has drawn pictures of her father and composed a piano piece to express her hope that he can gain freedom in China. And we thank her for coming forward to speak out in defense of her dad.

We will then hear from Mr. Chen Guangcheng via Skype who would have been here, but was not well enough to travel. As we all know he is a valiant Chinese human rights activist who worked on a variety of human rights issues especially the forced abortion issue. Blind from an early age and self taught in the law, Mr. Chen is frequently described as a barefoot lawyer who advocated for victims of forced abortion and sterilization and the welfare of the women and the poor and the disabled. He is best known for exposing massive abuses in official family planning policy, often involving violence and forced abortions. Imprisoned unjustly and tortured, first in prison and then under house arrest, he finally escaped house arrest in his rural town in east China, Shandong Province, and made it to the U.S. Embassy in Beijing, a legendary escape, the kind of stuff that super heroes are made of. The world watched and after negotiations, he was allowed to come to the U.S. and began a law fellowship at New York University. He recently became a distinguished senior fellow in human rights at the Witherspoon Institute in Princeton as well as distinguished visiting fellow at the Institute for Policy Research and Catholic Studies at the Catholic University of America and also a distinguished senior advisor at the Lantos Foundation for Human Rights and Justice.

We will then hear from Pastor Bob Fu who was a leader in the 1989 democracy movement in Tiananmen Square and later became a house church pastor and founder along with his wife. In 1996, authorities arrested Pastor Fu and imprisoned them for their work. After their release, they escaped to the United States in 2002, founded the ChinaAid Association. ChinaAid monitors and reports on religious freedom in China and provides a forum for discussion among experts on religion law and human rights in China. Pastor Fu is frequently interviewed by media outlets around the world. He has an incredible understanding of the Chinese dictatorship, but he also, amazingly, prays for not just the victims, but also for the tormentors and loves them both. Absolutely an amazing man.

We will then hear from T. Kumar who is the Amnesty International Director for International Advocacy and a very good friend of this subcommittee. He has testified before the U.S. Congress on numerous occasions to discuss human rights abuses around the world. He has served as a human rights monitor in many Asian countries as well as in Bosnia, Afghanistan, Guatemala, Sudan, and South Africa. He also served as director of several refugee ships and camps. T. Kumar was a political prisoner for over 5 years in Sri Lanka for his peaceful human rights activities. Amnesty International adopted him as a prisoner of conscience and now he does that for others and he does it so well. He started his legal studies in prison and eventually became an attorney at law and devoted his entire practice to defending political prisoners.

Ms. Zhang, if you would proceed.

STATEMENT OF MS. ZHANG QING, WIFE OF GUO FEIXIONG

[The following testimony was delivered through an interpreter.]

Ms. ZHANG. Honorable Chairman, Vice Chairman, Congressmen, and everyone here, I am the wife of Guo Feixiong. My name is

Zhang Qing. I am very thankful to every one of you to have this opportunity to introduce my husband's case to you, and also I am glad to tell you about my husband's activities in defending human rights, his ideals and personality, and his character.

In today's China, actually human rights continues to deteriorate. In the new round of government crackdowns on human rights movements, my husband has been detained for the fourth time. The charges were for motivating people for illegal gathering. In 2009, he publicly made a speech demanding for the freedom of expression in China. He believes that, in the West or in the East, the freedom of expression is the basic human right. There has never been any legal due process for my husband's case after he got arrested.

His lawyers and family members have been denied access to visit him, and it has been 83 days now. And we cannot see the end of this case. We don't know how long this will last. We don't know what will happen to him if the international community will not show their concern to this case. My husband, Guo Feixiong, was involved in the pro-democracy movement in 2003 and got arrested for the first time in 2005. In 2005, he was speaking out for the farmers who were losing their land because of government illegal seizure.

In 2006, he came to the States to attend a law conference. Many people actually advised him to stay in the United States, but when he looked at the democracy and freedom in this country, he made a commitment to bring back the ideals for freedom of expression and democracy back to the Chinese people. So he went back.

He was clearly aware of the possibility that he would be arrested again if he would return, but he still made the decision to return. It has been 10 years since the year, 2003, he got involved in pro-democracy movements. He has spent 5½ years in jail. He has always been the most frontier fighting for democracy movements. He does not only promote the theory of democracy movements, but actually he is a doer for these movements.

He has made a huge impact upon the pro-democracy movement in China. He has composed more than 40 articles summarizing and thinking about the pro-democracy movement in China. And it is because of all his activities that the government now is torturing him in jail. He has been in jail four times and has been tortured physically severely. Even other family members have been tortured as well.

One of the horrible tortures is that the policemen used electric rod to torture his genitals. They appealed to this torture to crack down, to crush his will for democracy and for freedom. But he will never change his commitment. So he will never surrender to such pressure and he is really, truly a model fighting for democracy and freedom.

He has been on a hunger strike for more than 100 days. He is regarded highly as a hero by the Chinese society as defending human rights.

In 2011, after 5 years being tortured in jail, but he continued his human rights activities asking Chinese Government to give back the freedom of expression to the Chinese people. And he organized a series of activities for the human rights cases. He asked the Chinese Government to approve the covenant of the human rights, that is the covenant of the United Nations and asking Chinese officials to publicly tell public their properties.

In 2006 and this year, in both crackdowns of the Chinese Government upon the human rights movement, and my husband Guo was the one that has been tortured mostly and has been treated illegally all the time. So I am here today to ask the Obama administration to speak on my husband's case. I ask the Obama administration and American officials to speak openly for my husband and ask the Chinese Government to release my husband without any condition.

I also appeal to American Congress that it is within your power and you can do something for my husband and to talk to the Chinese Government and to express your concern. And then to ask the Chinese Government to release my husband.

I also ask American Embassy to China to meet my husband because both lawyers and family members are denied the right to visit him.

America is the leading country for the human rights in this world. It serves as a lighthouse for the whole world. So the American administration and Congress have the obligation to support those who fight for human rights in China. So I also ask American administration and American Congress to talk and put pressure upon Chinese Government to release all those who are prisoners of conscience. Thank you.

[The prepared statement of Ms. Zhang follows:]

Hearing of the Committee on Foreign Affairs to be held by the Subcommittee on Africa, Global Health, Global Human Rights, and International Organizations in Room 2255 of the Rayburn House Office Building

DATE: Tuesday, October 29, 2013

TIME: 2:30 p.m.

SUBJECT: Guo Feixiong and Freedom of Expression in China

WITNESSES: Ms. Zhang Qing Wife of Guo Feixiong

Ms. Yang Tianjiao Daughter of Guo Feixiong

Pastor Bob Fu Founder and President ChinaAid Association

Mr. Chen Guangcheng

CHAIRMEN: Christopher H. Smith (R-NJ)

Zhang Qing

Honorable Chairman, Vice Chairman, Congressmen, and guests,

I'm thankful to have this opportunity to give you an introduction on my husband Guo Feixiong –his legal case, his activities in defending human rights, his ideals, his personality, and his character.

In China today, human rights conditions continue to deteriorate. In a new round of government crackdowns on civil movements this summer, my husband, Guo Feixiong, was detained again. This is his fourth time in prison within two years since he was released on September 13, 2011, after serving five years in prison on a false conviction.

Guo Feixiong was detained for the fourth time on August, 8, 2013. It wasn't until August 17, when his sister, Yang Maoping, received a notice of detention, that we learned that he was charged with "gathering a mob to disrupt the order of a public site." It was speculated that his detention was caused by his support of *The Southern Weekly* incident and the speech he delivered in public. He said in his speech, "China's system of censorship on books and newspapers is a censorship on people's thinking that free-thinkers and freedom fighters have strongly opposed since ancient times. This system should have been abolished long ago. We support *The Southern Weekly* today not just because it is being suppressed and persecuted. We need to rethink everything and fight for a universal right – freedom of speech. Freedom of speech releases the voice of hundreds of millions of people. It is an amplifier of citizens' power."

His attorney went to Tianhe detention center in Guangdong Province, requesting to meet with him, but was denied. So far his attorney has made seven requests to visit him, but all have been denied.

According to the law in China, detention should not exceed 37 days. After this period of time, the police must either release the litigant or issue an official arrest warrant to the litigant's family and lawyer. But the reality is that Guo Feixiong is still in detention, and neither his family nor lawyer has received an arrest warrant.

It wasn't until October 15, when his attorney submitted legal papers to the Tianhe Procuratorate to file a lawsuit, that the staff of the Parocuratorate said that Guo Feixiong had been officially arrested on September 12. On October 16, an official arrest warrant was delivered to Guo Feixiong's sister. These details show that someone behind the scenes orchestrated the whole process, including the timing of delivering legal papers to Guo Feixiong's family. Guo Feixiong's attorney commented that the Chinese authorities had "blatantly violated the law" in handling Guo Feixiong's case, which is manifested in Guo Feixiong's secret detention and secret arrest.

Guo Feixiong has been in detention for 78 days. The seven requests his attorney made to meet with him have all been denied. To this day, we still don't know his situation. This is a unique case of the authority's blatant violation of the law. We can't help but ask what the authorities are trying to cover up by unlawfully denying Guo Feixiong visits from his attorney? Is he suffering torture again or on a hunger strike protesting the government's illegal detention?

Guo Feixiong is a sincere believer of freedom and democracy – an idealist. He promotes the values and ideals of democracy and constitutionalism and practices his beliefs with actions. Since he started to participate in China's human rights defense activities in 2003, he has been at the front line of the citizens' rights defense movement for 10 years, serving the needs of the massive, marginalized people in society. Because of this kind of work, he was subjected to all kinds of brutal suppression, including four detainments, multiple beatings, and unlawful summons by the police. In 2006, because he was beat up, he, together with Gao Zhisheng, Fan Yafeng, and Zhao Xin, started a global hunger strike for defending rights. He wrote an article afterwards, *The Radicalness and Moderation of Relay Hunger Strike –the 3rd Commentary on the Global Relay Hunger Strike for Human Rights and against Violence*, highly regarding the significance of hunger strikes.

Later, July 2005, Guo Feixiong was hired as a legal advisor by villagers of the Taishi village, giving them legal assistance in their efforts to remove the corrupt village chief from office. The authorities responded to the villagers' legal request with a violent crackdown and many people were put in jail. Guo Feixiong was also seized and detained. He went on a hunger strike of 59 days to protest the government's illegal detention. Tao Jun, a democracy advocator, wrote in *A Look at the Chinese People's Rights Defense and Courage through Guo Feixiong*, "His multiple detainments are a result of his unyieldingness and a demonstration of his remarkable courage and decisiveness. His is one of the few true men who display the courage of the Chinese people, and they are a rare species in China today. His rights defense activities at Taishi village and his initiation of efforts to rescue Gao Zhisheng manifest his great courage and character. In spite of repeated persecutions, secret scheming by the government against him, and backstabbing from his peers, he remained unruffled and maintained his capacity to fight. His spirit of tenacity and persistence invites us to ponder. Courage has been eliminated to the edge of extinction in our nation, so his courage and braveness are as noble and precious as diamonds."

In an article about Guo Feixiong, Boxun News wrote, "The courage and the spirit of fighting have been wrung out of the blood of the Chinese people. Over several thousands of years, the Chinese people have nearly become boneless creatures through domestication: cowardly, withdrawn from the world, self-effacing, putting up with abuse, and without principles. Guo Feixiong's courage seems to have lit up this world of cowards." (http://www.boxun.com/news/gb/pubvp/2007/04/200704122336.shtml)

On August 5, 2006, Gao Zhisheng was arrested. Guo Feixiong organized rescue efforts with enthusiasm. As a result, he was subjected to the government's retaliation and was detained on September 14, 2006, on the charge of "illegal business activity" in connection with the publication of a book exposing political corruption, *Shenyang Political Earthquake*.

The authorities detained him without citing any material evidence and refused to release him based on the lack of facts against him. They brutally tortured him and transferred him from Guangzhou in southern China to Shenyang in northeastern China so as to use more brutal torture to crush his spirit and belief in the cause of freedom and democracy. They also used torture to create a false conviction and rip away his freedom.

Here is a list of abuses and tortures my husband went through:

1. He was interrogated for 13 days and nights nonstop and deprived of sleep at Guangzhou No.1 Detention Center.

2. Chains were put on his feet for more than 100 days at Guangzhou No. 1 Detention Center.

3. He was shackled to a wooden bed with his hands and feet crossed, unable to bend any part of his body, for 42 days at Guangzhou No. 1 Detention Center.

4. At Guangzhou No. 1 Detention Center, the police pulled his hair, tickled him, and insulted him for more than 20 days.

5. A black cover was put on his head, which is typically given to inmates on death row, after he was transferred to Shenyang. He was taken to a secret location for detention and suffered brutal beatings.

6. He was taken to a secret location for detention by Shenyang police and chained to a "tiger bench" for four hours.

7. At the secret location for detention in Shenyang, police hung him from the ceiling by his hands with only the strength of his shoulders to sustain his entire body weight.

8. At the secret location, police used an electric baton to electrocute his genitals.

9. Unable to bear the abuse of electrocuting his genitals, he attempted suicide by rushing towards glass windows.

10. Shenyang police locked him up with inmates on death row, who, in despair, threatened to gauge out Guo Feixiong's eyes. He was forced to fight back using glass from a window he smashed.

All the above are facts my husband presented in his final statement at the court.

Guo Feixiong's case was sent back to the Procuratorate for reinvestigation four times due to insufficient evidence, but eventually he was still sentenced to five years' imprisonment based on verbal confessions obtained by using the shameless torture of electrocuting his genitals. As his wife, I refuse to accept a false conviction fabricated through the use of shameless torture methods. For this reason, I wrote open letters to the Chinese President, U.S. President Bush, and the United Nations' Committee Against Torture to expose the torture my husband was subjected to. I also declared that I would go on a hunger strike every Wednesday until his release in protest against the Chinese government's use to torture on Guo Feixiong and the false conviction of five years' imprisonment.

The persecution of Guo Feixiong is not limited to him also, but also extended to his family and children. On the first day of Chinese New Year in 1996, we were tailed by a group of plainclothes and they took photos of our children, who were nine and four years old then. In prison, Guo Feixiong received this threat, "We'll not let your son enroll in elementary school, and we'll not let your daughter get into high school." They meant what they said. When I took my son to the headmaster of an elementary school to enroll him in the first grade, the headmaster said firmly, with my 6-year-old son present, "If I kick your child out of school, that'll be a violation of the law on education. If I refuse to accept your son as a student of our school, I'm not breaking any law."

My son was barred from school for a year. The next year, it was time for my daughter to enter high school. But no school would accept her. In fear, my daughter said to me in tears, "I don't want to stay at home with no school like my brother." My children's education was interfered with and controlled. These illegal practices made us feel completely insecure.

On September 13, 2011, Guo Feixiong was released from prison and he resumed his services for the disadvantaged people.

The rights defense activities he participated in include:

- Made public speeches and published articles in support of *The Southern Weekly*
- Organized and participated in the "Investigation into Li Wangyang's Death"
- Called on the National People's Congress to approve the International Covenant on Civil and Political Rights
- Demanded Chinese government officials to disclose their income to the public

Guo Feixiong participated in the 1986 student's movement of Shanghai and the 1989 nationwide students' movement. He is a sincere believer of freedom and democracy. Despite the brutal suppression he was subjected to, he refused to give up his convictions on freedom and democracy.

During the Chinese government's crackdown on rights defense movement in 2006, he suffered the severest torture and received the longest prison term. Gao Zhisheng was sentenced to three years, with a five-year probation. Hu Jia got three years and six months. Chen Guangcheng got four years and three months. Guo Feixiong got five years.

In a new round of government crackdown on civil movements this year, Guo Feixiong was dealt with illegally. He was secretly detained and secretly arrested, and has been denied attorney's visits to this day. People on the outside have no idea how he was detained and how he is doing at the detention center. We are concerned that he may be tortured. It is also possible that he is on a hunger strike in protest against the government's illegal detention of him, or there may be something else going on.

It wasn't until August 17 that people on the outside found out about Guo Feixiong's detention. *Global Times*, a government-sanctioned Chinese newspaper, issued an editorial on August 18, saying that this campaign launched by the government against human rights movement was named "Decapitation."

The family members and lawyers of those detained in this campaign were all notified about their detention in a timely manner according to normal procedures. The detained all met with their lawyers except Guo Feixiong, who was denied visits of his lawyer seven times.

Guo Feixiong sets a great example of someone who fights for freedom and human rights, does not fear mighty power, and does not submit to it. We often pray "lead us not into temptation" because we know the Devil's temptations are vicious and cruel and many people can't overcome them.

Guo Feixiong overcame temptations with his courage and his firm belief in freedom and democracy. The number of days he was on hunger strike totals 100 days. He has kept the baseline for this generation of people. He has always been considered a hero by pro-democracy activists.

I call on the international community and human rights organizations to supply moral support to Guo Feixiong, a warrior who is still fighting for human rights in darkness, affirm his sacrifice and his fighting spirit, and award him, so as to motivate more people to overcome fear and weakness and pursue human rights courageously.

Pro-democracy activists and scholars of China made this comment about Guo Feixiong: He is not only a theoretician, but also practices his theory. He has great influence on the development of civil and social movement. He values the development of civil society. He is good at drawing lessons from practices and applying them to other rights defense cases.

He has been at the frontline of civil movement for a decade and has been involved in many human rights defense activities both in theory and practice.

The Chinese government's response to Guo Feixiong's active involvement in the civil rights movement and his great influence is to give him the harshest suppression and persecution that they are able. The international community has not given attention and moral support in proportion to the persecution Guo Feixiong has suffered. We notice that the U.S. government voiced its support to other activists arrested in the same period of time as Guo Feixiong's arrest. Up to this point, Guo Feixiong has not been mentioned officially by the U.S. Department of State even though three weeks ago, I met with the acting Assistant Secretary of State and asked the U.S. government to make a public statement in support of Guo Feixiong's release. It is a pity we haven't seen that public statement being made. Today, I would like to make the following appeals to the U.S. government and Congress:

1. I call on President Obama and the U.S. Department of State to publicly mention Guo Feixiong's name and make a public statement in support of Guo Feixiong's innocence and release.

2. I ask the U.S. Congress to communicate with the Chinese authorities through the passing of a resolution or other effective means, expressing its strong concern for Guo Feixiong's case and promoting and supporting his release. He is innocent. All he did is to promote the rule of law and human rights in China. Nothing he did has violated the law.

3. The U.S. Ambassador to China and the U.S. Consulate General in Guangzhou should ask the Chinese government for permission to meet with Guo Feixiong since he was denied visits from his attorney seven times.

The United States is a primary champion of human rights in the world and serves as a beacon for the global human rights movement. Therefore, the U.S. President, the U.S. State Department, and the U.S. Congress have the responsibility to speak up for and render moral support to Chinese human rights activist Guo Feixiong who has been persecuted for his work. I also call on the U.S. government and Congress to put pressure on the Chinese government, urging it to release all the prisoners detained for political reasons, conscience, and religious reasons.

Mr. SMITH. Thank you so very much for that extraordinarily powerful testimony and we will follow up. We will do a letter. We will include the entirety of this hearing record to President Obama, to Secretary Kerry, and to Ambassador Gary Locke, our Ambassador to People's Republic of China and other interested parties within the administration and we will contact the Chinese ourselves as a committee. So thank you for those very tangible follow-up things for us to do. I do have questions for later, but now we'll go to Ms. Yang.

STATEMENT OF MS. YANG TIANJIAO, DAUGHTER OF GUO FEIXIONG

Ms. YANG. Dear Honorable Chairman, Members of Congress, and friends, my name is Yang Tianjiao and my American name is Sara. My dad is Guo Feixiong. I am here to thank the Congress and Congressman Smith for giving me this opportunity to speak here.

The last time I saw my dad was about 7 years ago. It was in 2006, and I was only 10. I remember that he brought me this video game, and we played it almost every day during that summer. However, on September 14th, when I came back from school, he was gone, and I have not seen him since that day. I did not even have a chance to say "Bye" or "I love you" to him.

Over the past 7 years, I have dreamed about him a lot. I dreamed that he would play that video game with me again so we could pass level 5 together. But they were only dreams. The next day I always found myself in tears.

I got to know about my dad's condition from my mom's conversation with friends. My mom would not talk about my dad's news in front of me because she thought it was too heavy for a 10-year-old girl to accept. But I still listened to them anyway, and to be honest, they were extremely heavy, sad, and shocking. I heard that he was incarcerated for 5 years. During those 5 years, the government transferred him to many different places and used numerous different tortures against him. I was always so deeply hurt when I heard about them.

In 2009, we moved to the United States of America. In 2011, my dad got out of jail. The day he was out, we talked on the phone. I literally cried when I heard his voice. I had been longing to hear this voice for 5 years, and I could finally do that.

Over the past 2 years, I talked to my dad through Skype. He gave me advice for life, and I showed him my artwork. A few years ago, I drew my dad in a miniature cartoon form, and he immediately complained about the one short leg and one long leg when he saw it. Recently, my art skills have improved so much that he applauded my artwork. However, he still pushes me to move forward; he still wants me to draw like some of the most famous and brilliant artists like Da Vinci, Michelangelo, et cetera.

But the good times did not last long. He was captured, again, on August 8th, 2013. That hurt. That day was Father's Day in China. Again, I do not remember our last conversation. Again, I did not get to say a formal goodbye to him. Again, I have not heard his voice for about 70 days. Again, I miss him so much.

Right now, I have a watercolor painting of my dad that I finished in September. I am sorry I did not bring it today. I hang it on my wall so that I can see his face every day. In this painting, he is smiling. In my memory that is what he looked like every day when we were together. Also, I composed a piano piece called ''The Cosmos.'' This is a piece for my dad. I would always laugh at my dad when he joked that he fell asleep to my piano playing.

However, words, drawings, and music cannot express how much I miss him. My dad is a great man; he is my hero. He has helped so many people. He, a man who pursues democracy, works so hard to improve the law of China. I, his daughter, always want my dad to have the freedom that he works so hard to achieve for others. I always want him to be safe and free.

President Obama, you also have two daughters; you are also a human rights lawyer. I wish that President Obama can send a request to China to free my father. I do not know what has happened to him in jail for the past 2 months. I am so worried about his health, so I hope that the Congress will talk to the Chinese Government and secure my father's freedom.

Thank you very much.

[The prepared statement of Ms. Yang follows:]

Hearing of the Committee on Foreign Affairs to be held by the Subcommittee on Africa, Global Health, Global Human Rights, and International Organizations in Room 2255 of the Rayburn House Office Building

DATE: Tuesday, October 29, 2013

TIME: 2:30 p.m.

SUBJECT: Guo Feixiong and Freedom of Expression in China

WITNESSES: Ms. Zhang Qing Wife of Guo Feixiong

Ms. Yang Tianjiao Daughter of Guo Feixiong

Pastor Bob Fu Founder and President ChinaAid Association

Mr. Chen Guangcheng

CHAIRMEN: Christopher H. Smith (R-NJ)

Testimony before Subcommittee on Africa, Health and Global Human Rights of the House Foreign Affairs Committee

By Tianjiao "Sara" Yang

Dear Honorable Chairman, members of Congress, and friends,

My name is Yang Tianjiao and my American name is Sara. My dad is Guo Feixiong. I am here to thank the Congress and Congressman Smith for giving me this opportunity to speak here.

The last time I saw my dad was about 7 years ago. It was in 2006, and I was only 10. I remember that he bought me this video game, and we played it almost every day during that summer. However, on September 14th, when I came back from school, he was gone, and I have not seen him since that day. I did not even have a chance to say "bye" or "I love you" to him.

Over the past 7 years, I have dreamed about him a lot. I dreamed that he would play that video game with me again so we could pass level 5 together. But they were only dreams. The next day I always found myself in tears.

I got to know about my dad's condition from my mom's conversations with her friends. My mom would not talk about my dad's news in front of me because she thought it was too heavy for a 10-year-old girl to accept. But I still listened to them anyway, and to be honest, they were extremely heavy, sad, and shocking. I heard that he was incarcerated for five years. During those five years, the government transferred him to many different places and used numerous different tortures to against him. I was always so deeply hurt when I heard about them.

In 2009, we moved to the United States of America. In 2011, my dad got out of jail. The day he was out, we talked on the phone. I literally cried when I heard his voice. I had been longing to hear this voice for five years, and I could finally do that.

Over the past two years, I talked to my dad through Skype. He gave me advice for life, and I showed him my drawings. A few years ago, I drew my dad in a miniature cartoon form, and he immediately complained about the one short leg and one long leg when he saw it. Recently, my art skills have improved so much that he applauded my artwork. However, he still pushes me to move forward; he still wants me to draw like some of the most famous and brilliant artists–Da Vinci, Michelangelo, etc.

But the good times did not last long. He was captured, again, on August 8th, 2013. Again, I do not remember our last conversation. Again, I did not get to say a formal "goodbye" to him. Again, I have not heard his voice for about 70 days. Again, I miss him so much.

Right now, I have a water color painting of my dad that I finished in September. I hang it on my wall so that I can see his face every day. In this painting, he is smiling. In my memory that is what he looked like every day when we were together. Also, I composed a piano piece called "The Cosmos." This is a piece for my dad. I would always laugh at him when he joked that he fell asleep to my piano playing.

However, words, drawings, and music cannot express how much I miss him. My dad is a great man; he is my hero. He has helped so many people. He, a man who pursues democracy, works so hard to improve the law of China. I, his daughter, always want my dad to have the freedom that he works so hard to achieve for others. I always want him to be safe and free. President Obama, you also have two daughters; you are also a human-right lawyer. I wish that President Obama can send a request to China to free my father. I do not know what has happened to him in jail for the past two months. I am so worried about his health, so I hope that the Congress will talk to the Chinese government and secure my father's freedom!

Thank you very much!!

"Sara" Yang Tianjiao

Mr. SMITH. Ms. Yang, thank you so very much for that testimony. Tears, deep hurt, and the watercolor painting of him smiling on your wall. Those are so touching and I hope that the President, the Vice President, our own leadership here in the House and Senate will act. We certainly will as a subcommittee. We will do everything we can to secure your father's release and your testimony is so moving. No one can hear that and not be moved. So thank you, and to your mom as well.

We do have some difficulties still, but we are going to have to switch to audio only although we will keep the visual as long as we can to hear the great Chen Guangcheng testify. So I would like now to yield to Mr. Chen. Hearing no objection, we will just go to audio and we will proceed.

Bob Fu will now use a cell phone in a way that he did twice when Mr. Chen was in a hospital under arrest. He couldn't leave obviously. The hospital room was filled with Chinese police. Bob Fu got through to him and that is where he made his famous appeal to come to the United States, and within hours he was given approval.

STATEMENT OF MR. CHEN GUANGCHENG, CHINESE HUMAN RIGHTS ACTIVIST (APPEARING VIA VIDEOCONFERENCE)

[The following testimony was delivered through an interpreter via cell phone.]

Mr. CHEN. Dear Honorable Chairman, honorable members of the human rights subcommittee and friends, greetings to all of you.

Human rights fighter Mr. Guo Feixiong has been detained for 83 days now. It has been eight times that the Chinese Government has denied his basic rights to see a lawyer. This is a clear violation of Chinese own laws and citizens' basic civil rights. We have no idea whether he is alive or he is dead.

In 2005, Guo Feixiong, Gao Zhisheng, and I were persecuted by the Chinese Government almost at the same time. And today, Gao Zhisheng is still in jail and his family members are forbidden to visit him. Guo Feixiong was arrested again only after he was released less than 2 years ago from his last imprisonment. So today, the communist party is showing the whole world it has no idea to change and will continue to fight against human rights. So we shouldn't have any illusions toward the Chinese Communist Party any more.

The trial of Ms. Liu Ping, Mr. Wei Zhongping and Li Sihua in Jiangxi yesterday is deemed by the citizens in China as the evil trials against the good. In the name of social stability maintenance, a number of citizens, petitioners, and activists were kidnapped, tortured, and arrested. The lawyers who were supposed to represent the three activists on trial were forced to cancel their legal contract with their clients because they couldn't meet up with their clients.

A report released by the Freedom House last week shows the crackdown against freedom of speech, Internet freedom, and media censorship in China has already extended beyond China's borders. This crackdown actually started this spring and since then more than 150 people got arrested. The communist regime is really only using this trial against these three activists in Jiangxi as a test to the international community to see how we will respond, and then

I believe it will get worse and worse if we don't respond to take the proper actions. In his first arrest, Guo Feixiong was tortured severely. So this should really concern and worry everyone this time because he has been arrested for so long without any legal rights, and his lawyers and family members cannot visit him.

And the freedom belongs to the brave people. And this illegal trial against these three innocent Chinese citizens really occasioned the strongest protest among the Chinese people. Nobody's rights will be guaranteed without a sound system. It is my hope that the United States of America and the international community will help assist the Chinese people in getting onto the path of freedom, democracy, and constitutionalism as soon as possible.

The most urgent task before us is to achieve Internet freedom in China. The communist regime right now is undermining Internet freedom and restricts the free access of information. Internet censorship is overwhelming and a large number of Internet policemen are hired to censor, block, and delete postings online which is a blatant violation of the Universal Declaration of Human Rights according to Article 19. This article states that everyone has the right to seek, receive, and impart information and ideas through any media and regardless of frontiers.

Hillary Clinton once stated clearly that the policy of the United States is to support an Internet that allows every human being equal access to knowledge, to thoughts, and dedicating itself to the promotion of Internet freedom. If this policy of the United States can truly be implemented, that will be a great contribution to the freedom in China as well as to the whole world. So right now it is high time we provide assistance to the freedom-loving people in totalitarian countries and tear down the Internet version of the Berlin Wall.

Therefore, I suggest to all Congress and administration for every free nation to increase their funding to help develop some software so that we can break through firewalls such as FOE, Freegate, or Ultrasurf, which are all very effective. I learned that the U.S. Congress has a $700 million budget for this purpose, but only less than 3 percent is spent on breaking through China's firewalls. Therefore, it is very urgent for Congress to increase the budget for the Internet freedom in China.

Secondly, it is my suggestion that the judicial and administrative organs must join hands in establishing a mechanism for human rights violators and it is hoped that we can stop them, set up a global database of human rights violators, including the ''610 Office'' of the Chinese Communist Party and the Family Planning Commission at all levels of government. Expand, establish, and strictly implement current laws similar to the Magnitsky Act, which prohibits the entrance of Russian human rights violators into the United States. And we need to freeze their assets in the United States and abroad, putting an end to the history of those vicious officials when they can enjoy the freedom overseas, like in America, while exercising their tyranny in their home country.

So we need to set up a trans-congressional human rights alliance of free countries and convene regularly and invite civilians, human rights defenders, victims, their family members, and authorized agents to share their stories.

So the people in the free world, we need to speak up and stand up for all those human rights fighters and to show our concern and to invite them to join hands and fight together.

Fourthly, we need to demand the Chinese Communist Party to stop persecuting religious believers and respect religious freedom. One hundred and twenty Tibetan monks have immolated themselves. People in Xinjiang fighting against tyranny have been shot one after another. And we all know the persecution of Falun Gong practitioners as well as those underground house church Christians. They are all suffering from persecution. All the groups mentioned above, they all can get along with other Asians, Europeans, and Americans and earn their respect, yet why can't the Chinese Communist regime tolerate them?

Fifthly, I call on lawyers and legal experts of the United States and the American Bar Association to advocate for human rights lawyers of China and make joint efforts to provide them with some specific legal support and assistance.

Sixthly, I hope the annual U.S.-China Human Rights Dialogue will be practical in advancing human rights and dare to be open and honest. Human rights dialogues should not become a matter of formality and empty talk.

And last, I also want to appeal to American people—and you voted all those officials and congressmen into office, so I appeal to you that you will talk to your congressmen and officials and apply all resources and means to help terminate China's evil one-child policy and forced abortion. Because to force women to abort their babies is a violation of universal human rights. It tramples on women's rights, the right of free choice, and also the sacred right of life. This wicked policy results in a severe imbalance in gender ratio and a rapidly aging population. So I plead earnestly with you kind-hearted American people to take actions right away. Contact your representatives and officials and ask them to show their concern to all the issues that is discussed above. Thank you, Chairman. Thank you, all the members of the human rights subcommittee, and thank you, everyone present at this hearing.

[The prepared statement of Mr. Chen follows:]

Hearing of the Committee on Foreign Affairs to be held by the Subcommittee on Africa, Global Health, Global Human Rights, and International Organizations in Room 2255 of the Rayburn House Office Building

DATE: Tuesday, October 29, 2013

TIME: 2:30 p.m.

SUBJECT: Guo Feixiong and Freedom of Expression in China

WITNESSES: Ms. Zhang Qing Wife of Guo Feixiong

Ms. Yang Tianjiao Daughter of Guo Feixiong

Pastor Bob Fu Founder and President ChinaAid Association

Mr. Chen Guangcheng

CHAIRMEN: Christopher H. Smith (R-NJ)

Mr. Chen Guangcheng

Dear honorable Chairman, honorable members of the committee and friends,

Greetings.

The detention of brave human rights leader Mr. Guo Feixiong has lasted for over 83 days for practicing his civil rights. During this time the regime has denied access to his lawyers eight times already. This is a clear violation of Chinese laws and citizens' basic civil rights. So, whether Guo is alive or dead is unknown.

In 2005, Guo Feixiong, Gao Zhisheng and I were persecuted by the Chinese regime almost simultaneously. Now, Gao Zhisheng is still in prison and his family members are forbidden to meet with him. Guo Feixiong was arrested again after being released less than two years ago from his last imprisonment. These events show the Chinese Communist Party (CCP) is determined to fight against human rights and rule of law, and we should not have any illusions toward the CCP regime anymore.

The trial of Ms. Liu Ping, Mr. Wei Zhongping and Li Sihua in Jiangxi yesterday was deemed by netizens as the evil against the good. In the name of social stability maintenance, a number of citizens, petitioners, and activists were kidnapped, tortured, and arrested. The lawyers who represent the three activist citizens on trial in Jiangxi were forced to cancel their legal contract with their clients.

A report released by the Freedom House last week shows the crackdown against freedom of speech, Internet freedom, and media censorship in China has already extended beyond China's borders. Nearly 150 people were already arrested since the crackdown started this spring. The CCP is using the trial against the three activists in Jiangxi as a test to the international community. If we don't take actions, things will become worse. When Guo Feixiong was imprisoned last time he was tortured severely. It is certainly worrisome this time as Guo's lawyer and family have not been allowed to meet with him so far.

Freedom belongs to brave people. The extraordinary reaction against the illegal trial of three innocent citizen activists in Jiangxin province yesterday shows that the trial itself is against citizens' will. Nobody's rights will be guaranteed without a system safeguard. I hope the United States of America and the international community assist the Chinese people in getting onto the path of freedom, democracy, and constitutionalism as soon as possible.

The most urgent task now is to achieve Internet freedom because the Chinese communist authorities undermine Internet freedom and restrict the free access of information. Internet censorship is overwhelming and a large number of Internet management agents are hired to censor, block, and delete postings online, which is a blatant violation of the Universal Declaration of Human Rights since according to Article 19 of the Declaration, everyone has the right to seek, receive, and impart information and ideas through any media and regardless of frontiers.

Hillary Clinton once stated clearly the policy of the U.S. government, which includes supporting an Internet that allows all the members of human race equal access to knowledge and thoughts and dedicating itself to the promotion of Internet freedom. The successful implementation of this policy of the United States will be vital to Internet freedom in China as well as the world. It is time to move forward to provide assistance to the freedom-loving people in totalitarian countries and tear down the Internet version of the Berlin Wall.

I suggest the legislative and administrative organs of each free nation increase government funding to encourage the research, development, and distribution of software that breaks through firewalls, such as FOE, Freegate, or Ultrasurf, which are all very effective. I learned that the U.S. Congress has a 700 million dollar budget for this, but only less than 3% is spent on breaking through China's firewalls. It is urgent to increase the budget for the Internet freedom in China.

Secondly, judicial and administrative organs must join hands in establishing a deterrent mechanism for human rights violators. Set up a global database of human rights violators, including the "610 Office" of the Chinese Communist Party and the Family Planning Commission at all levels of government. Expand, establish, and strictly implement current laws similar to the Magnitsky Act which prohibits the entrance of Russian rights-violating officials into the United States. Freeze their assets in the U.S. and abroad. Put an end to the history of wicked officials enjoying freedom overseas while exercising tyranny in their home country.

Thirdly, set up a trans-congressional human rights alliance of free countries. Convene regularly and invite civilians, human rights defenders, victims, their families, and authorized agents to share their stories.

Fourthly, demand that the CCP stop persecuting religious believers and respect religious freedom. One hundred twenty Tibetan monks have immolated themselves. People in

Xinjiang fighting against tyranny have been shot one after another. And we all know the indescribable persecution Falun Gong practitioners have suffered. These ethnic and religious groups can get along with other Asians, Europeans, and Americans, and earn their respect, yet why can the Chinese Communist government not tolerate them?

Fifthly, I call on lawyers and legal experts of the United States and the American Bar Association to advocate for the human rights lawyers of China and make joint efforts to provide them with some specific legal support and assistance.

Sixthly, I hope the annual U.S.-China Human Rights Dialogue will be practical in advancing human rights and dare to be open and honest. Human rights dialogues should not become a matter of formality and empty talk.

And last, I would like to call on the American people to take actions to urge the officials and congressmen you voted into office to apply all resources and means to help terminate China's evil one-child policy and forcible abortion because forcing women to abort their babies is a violation of universal human rights. It tramples on women's rights, the right of free choice, and also the sacred right of life. This wicked policy results in a severe imbalance in gender ratio and a rapidly aging population. I plead earnestly with you, kind-hearted American people, to take actions right now to contact your representatives and officials through text message, Twitter, Facebook, and other means, asking for their support on the human rights issues mentioned above. Caring for and supporting human rights is caring for and supporting ourselves, our children, and the generations to come.

Thank you.

Chen Guangcheng

Mr. SMITH. Mr. Chen, thank you very much for your eloquent testimony and for your very detailed list of actionable items. I wonder will you be able to stay with us or do you have to go?

Mr. CHEN. Yes, I can stay.

Mr. SMITH. Thank you. We will have questions after our final two witnesses.

Mr. SMITH. Mr. Fu, the floor is yours.

STATEMENT OF PASTOR BOB FU, FOUNDER AND PRESIDENT, CHINAAID ASSOCIATION

Mr. FU. Thank you, Mr. Chairman, and thank you for your years of leadership and support for this very important cause for freedom not only in China, but also globally as a voice for this voiceless and for this oppressed people.

Today, when I entered into this room I felt both gladly and sadly. I am glad that we still have congressional leaders like you, like other members, who are still concerned and support this cause, although it is not a popular cause anymore, with the decline of economic prosperity and economic stake in the global forum.

I am sad because 4 years after Guo Feixiong's wife and two children were able to come to the United States and we're still talking about Guo Feixiong's freedom. I still remember in 2009 in a small hotel in Bangkok, I flew there because I heard Ms. Zhang Qing with her two kids had to escape from China because they could not live a normal life anymore when Guo Feixiong was in prison, was tortured and the kids could not even find opportunity to get their education. The wife could not even find a right job for her. Increasing incredible obstacles including the denial of refugee status from the United Nations, including refusal to help by the U.S. Government officials, and I already booked my return flight to the United States. I was waiting to continue to file petition or appeal to the U.N., but seeing and looking in the eyes of these two kids, including Ms. Yang, Sara, who is sitting next to me, full of reluctance and fear, and seeing, watching that little boy, was playing with me and really begging me to stay with him to play with him. I just could not leave them behind.

Of course, as a friend and fellow freedom fighter, I would not leave his family members behind by coming back alone even if that means I have to take what some people call radical procedures, between the letter of the law and my own conscience. So I took them to the United States with some extraordinary procedures, which is written in my memoir, "God's Double Agent."

I was happy to see the family finally need not worry about what would happen in the middle of the night, what would happen to the two kids when they walk in the darkness on the road to do shopping, what would happen to their dad in the middle of the night when they woke up.

Of course, I want to thank many leaders of this country, especially many citizens in the great State of Texas, where I have been residing since 2004, and even today several members of the business community, religious community, flew all the way from Texas to come here to show their solidarity and their support for the freedom of Guo Feixiong. I want to recognize them. They are in the midst of this hearing. I want to especially thank Mr. Joe Torres, who is here as the chairman of the board of ChinaAid, as business leader, CPA. Of course, now the tax season is approaching and we all know this sacrifice he has encountered for engaging the ministry of ChinaAid by helping these families like Mr. Guo's family.

I want to thank Pastor Chad Bullard, who was a former official of Homeland Security Department, now a pastor of 6,000-member church who came here also to support the family where the Guo family are members of that church, Stonegate Fellowship.

I also want to thank Pastor Daniel Stevens, on my left, who is my pastor and my fellow co-worker at Mid-Cities Community Church. I still remember that very day when I heard mother and children were wandering on the street. It was Guo Feixiong's family. I wanted to fly there immediately to Bangkok to comfort them, to find a place to stay, but we don't have a budget. So I just emailed Pastor Daniel. I said, could you help. Without hesitation, not a single question even was asked. The next day I was able to buy the most expensive air tickets, $5,000 to get to Bangkok, that enabled me to meet with these family members and comfort them and situate them in a hotel room.

Mr. Chairman and members of this subcommittee, since the beginning of this year, the environment for freedom of speech in China has rapidly worsened. The Chinese Communist authorities have launched a campaign across China to strictly purge opinions voiced on the Internet and other peaceful public forums.

Mr. Guo Feixiong's arrest was just one of the cases of arbitrary arrest. The official propaganda of the Chinese Communists severely criticized the democratic constitutional trains of thought. Besides, the Communist Party also severely suppressed the new civil citizen movement. According to incomplete statistics, from the protest incident to other peaceful petitioning, at least over 100 people across China, some even respected writers, estimated it may be thousands of Chinese citizens have been arrested for simply expressing themselves or for peaceful petitioning in front of the government.

There has been a huge increase in the number of cyber police officers in China. The Golden Shield Project, the so-called Great Firewall of China, strictly shield overseas Web sites that the Chinese Communists think are sensitive, and many netizens have been summoned or detained just because they talked about civil society, the constitutionalism, and they gathered in the same city and talk about the word democracy in their QQ chatting forums. The Chinese Government has trained 2 million Web moderators or censors to delete posted messages and to ''guide public opinion.''

In the past 4 months, the Chinese Communist Government has arrested public intellectuals, influential, even business leaders such as Yang Xiuyu, Zhou Lubao, Fu Xuesheng, and Dong Liangje, who is an environmentalist. So the purpose of this operation by the Chinese Communists is to warn and punish those influential public intellectuals so that the ordinary netizens will not dare to voice their opinions on political and social issues.

And furthermore, it seems the Chinese Government tries to legalize and legitimize by the court system and the prosecution system all these crackdowns. And there is a joint document issued so-called ''Interpretation on Several Questions on the Applicable Law on Criminal Cases of Utilizing the Internet for Slandering.'' So nowadays, if the government or any police deemed a citizen who just used the Chinese version of Twitter to forward a message for public knowledge or raising the public awareness, if the forwarding has hit over 5,000 hits, it is called a case of "serious circumstances that constitutes the crime of slandering." It is a crime for prosecution.

Of course, there are a number of other arrests in suppressing those people who freely express themselves and peacefully fight for civil rights and those public intellectuals such as Dr. Xu Zhiyong, such as a billionaire who supports the freedom of expression, Mr. Wang Gongquan, such as Yuan Dong, such as Zhang Baocheng, such as Hou Xin, such as Ma Xinli. They were all arrested for simply making their opinion known without even taking much action on the street.

Of course, the end of April, Ms. Liu Ping, Wei Zhongping, and Li Sihua of Xinyu City, Jiangxi Province whose trial was abruptly finished yesterday because of the arbitrary trial and basically the government assigned all these illegal procedures. And the lawyers had to withdraw themselves.

So we have seen this since President Xi Jinping took power, the Chinese Government has become more severe in suppressing the rights defenders, restricting the freedom of speech, and in controlling the society.

Of course, in other areas like the rule of law, like the religious freedom have also been worsened. So every day in China, there are thousands of incidents of forced demolition of houses and every year thousands or millions of people's properties are violated. As a result, there are dozens of millions of petitioners in China, many of them were forced into the "Black jails" which resulted in numerous occasions of torture and rape of women.

The Chinese Communist Government continues to severely suppress the house churches. Of course, since April of this year, there are more Christians who have faced prosecution and received criminal sentence than the combination of the whole year last year. That has been happening from Henan Province to Inner Mongolia. And the house church Christians were sentenced from 2 years' to 7 years' imprisonment for simply organizing a peaceful worship service in their own homes.

What has aroused the most concern recently is the incident in which Peking University dismissed Associate Professor Xia Yeliang, which shows the position of the Chinese Government in strictly controlling the freedom of speech. Professor Xia promoted China's reform toward democratic constitutionalism on the Internet. So the Peking University simply dismissed him.

It is sad for us that the status of human rights and rule of law in China is seriously disconcerting. Without human dignity or basic human rights, the modernization of China is worthless. On the contrary, when China is headed toward the opposite direction of universal values, this doubtlessly poses a greater and greater threat to America and to the civilized world.

I think China, instead of suppressing these brave soldiers for freedom, civil society, and democracy, should embrace them, these individuals like my friend Guo Feixiong, like my friend, Gao Zhisheng, like many others for still sitting in the dark prison such for simply hoping and advancing the very freedom that every human being are cherishing. I think they should be awarded. I think they should be embraced by the Chinese Government, certainly the Chinese people. That will make the 21st century a safer and better and much greater place for us to stay. Thank you, Mr. Chairman.

[The prepared statement of Mr. Fu follows:]

Hearing of the Committee on Foreign Affairs to be held by the Subcommittee on Africa, Global Health, Global Human Rights, and International Organizations in Room 2255 of the Rayburn House Office Building

DATE: Tuesday, October 29, 2013

TIME: 2:30 p.m.

SUBJECT: Guo Feixiong and Freedom of Expression in China

WITNESSES: Ms. Zhang Qing Wife of Guo Feixiong

Ms. Yang Tianjiao Daughter of Guo Feixiong

Pastor Bob Fu Founder and President ChinaAid Association

Mr. Chen Guangcheng

CHAIRMEN: Christopher H. Smith (R-NJ)

The Chinese Government is Severely Suppressing Dissident Leaders. The Environment for Freedom of Speech Continues to Worsen.

Pastor Bob Fu, president of China Aid Association.

Since the beginning of this year, the environment for freedom of speech in China has rapidly worsened. The Chinese Communist authorities have launched a campaign across China to strictly purge opinions voiced on the Internet. Meanwhile, the official propaganda of the Chinese Communists severely criticizes democratic constitutional trains of thought. Besides, the Communist government also severely suppresses the new civil movement. According to incomplete statistics, from the protest incident of INFZM.com of Nanfang Daily until now, over 100 people across China have been arrested for expressing themselves or for peaceful petitioning.

Mr. Guo Feixiong was secretly arrested under such a circumstance. Guo Feixiong is a prominent dissident and a rights defender in China. In the past 10 years, he has been illegally detained and arrested many times. On November 12, 2007, he was sentenced to five years by the Chinese Communists. During his detention, he was tortured and mistreated many times. The direct reason for Guo Feixiong's arrest this August is his participation in the peaceful protest by INFZM.com of Nanfang Daily at the beginning of this year. He delivered a speech to the crowd calling on the government officials to make public the value of their properties and calling for freedom of speech and freedom of press. His lawyer's requests to meet with Guo Feixiong were rejected six times by the Public Security agency.

Let me elaborate on three aspects that prove that the human rights status in China continues to worsen and the space for freedom of speech is further condensed.

1. The Chinese Communist government is reorganizing and strictly controlling the Internet.
There has been a huge increase in the number of cyberpolice officers in China. The Golden Shield Project and the Great Firewall of China strictly shield overseas websites that the Chinese Communists think are sensitive, and they filter a large amount of information. The socializing tools of the Chinese citizens such as email, Microblog, QQ, Skype, Wechat, etc., have been under surveillance. Many netizens have been summoned or detained just because they talked about civil society, gatherings in the same city, constitutionalism and democracy in their QQ chatting lounges or emails. The Chinese government has trained two million web moderators to delete posted messages and to "guide public opinion." Such a system of selective and unilateral indoctrination of information is a typical means by which an autocratic society monopolizes information and controls people's mind.

In the past four months, the Chinese Communists have arrested some influential people in their exclusive operation called "reorganizing and cracking down on web rumors," such as Xue Biqun (net name: Xue Manzi) who has 12 million fans, Qin Zhihui (net name: Qin Huohuo), Yang Xiuyu (net name: Lisanchaisi), Zhou Lubao, Fu Xuesheng, Dong Liangjie (important environmentalists), and Dong Rubin (net name: Bianmin). The purpose of this operation by the Chinese Communists is to warn and punish those influential public intellectuals so that the ordinary netizens will not dare to voice their opinions on political and social issues that the Chinese Communists think are sensitive.

For this purpose, the Supreme People's Court and the Supreme People's Procuratorate in China jointly issued "Interpretation on Several Questions on the Applicable Law on Criminal Cases of Utilizing the Internet for Slandering." The judicial interpretation clearly stipulates: "Those who utilize the Internet to slander other people and whose slandering information has over 5,000 hits or whose information has been transferred for over 500 times would fit in the case of 'serious circumstance that constitutes the crime of slandering' as stipulated in Clause 1 of Article 246 of the Criminal Law of the People's Republic of China. The publication of this regulation has caused hundreds of millions of netizens to fear freely expressing themselves. There are no ways for the Chinese people to get true and complete information and to truly express their own opinions and publish their comments on public issues that concern them.

2. The Chinese Communists severely suppress people who freely express themselves and peacefully fight for civil rights.

A group of public intellectuals with a sense of social responsibility and citizens who are fighting for basic human rights are being cracked down on by the Chinese Communist government.

Several dozens of these citizens have been arrested and will face sentencing for calling on the government officials to make public the value of their properties, for calling for the implementation of constitutional democracy and free elections and for fighting for equality in the right to receive education.

Dr. Xu Zhiyong, an instructor at Beijing University of Posts and Telecommunications and the former head of Open Constitution Initiative, was placed on criminal detention on July 16, 2013, on the charge of "gathering a mob to disrupt the order of a public place" because he called for the establishment of a civil society and equality in the right to education. On August 23, he was officially arrested. Mr. Wang Gongquan, a famous investor in China who is enthusiastic in public good and who called for actions of new citizens and equality in the right to education was placed on criminal detention on the same charge as Xu Zhiyong. He was officially arrested last week.

In March, Yuan Dong, Zhang Baocheng, Hou Xin, Ma Xinli and other citizens totaling 10 people drew a banner in Xidan, Beijing asking the government officials to make public the value of their properties. They were placed under criminal detention. After that, several dozens of citizens from Guangzhou in the south through Harbin in the north have been arrested for going into the streets calling for the government officials to make public the value of their properties. On April 17, Mr. Zhao Changqing, a prominent Christian dissident, was arrested in Beijing. He was arrested only because he peacefully unfolded a banner in a street in Beijing demanding that the government officials make public the value of their properties. Ding Jiaxi, a rights defense attorney, was arrested with the same charge.

At the end of April, Liu Ping, Wei Zhongping, and Li Sihua of Xinyu City, Jiangxi Province were arrested for publicly calling for free elections. The case was tried in court yesterday. The dissident Zhang Lin was arrested on July 28 for publicly protesting against the local government for depriving his daughter of her right to attend schools. This is the fifth time he has been arrested. On August 10, Li Huaping, a web writer in Shanghai, was arrested for calling for the citizens in the same city to gather together. On September 3, Yao Cheng, a rights defender in Anhui, was arrested by the police for fighting for Zhang Lin's 10-year-old daughter's right to attend schools. According to incomplete statistics, in half a year, over 100 people across China have been arrested for freely expressing themselves or for peacefully gathering together to protest.

We see from this that since Mr. Xi Jinping took power, the Chinese government has become more severe in suppressing the rights defenders, restricting the freedom of speech and in controlling the society.

3. The status of human rights continues to worsen and the rule of law has suffered a retrogression.

Due to the growth of the Internet, the number of netizens in China is already nearly 600 million. There is no way that the Chinese Communists can completely block information and control public opinions as they used to do in the past. On the one hand, the corruption of the Chinese Communist officials has reached a high point rarely seen in history and the conflicts between the officials and the general public are becoming more and more intense. On the other hand, the general public has experienced an awakening in their consciousness of civil rights and human rights. The great masses all call on the Chinese Communists to launch political reforms, implement democratic constitutionalism as soon as possible and protect basic human rights from being violated.

To keep social stability and consolidate its own power, the Chinese Communists disregard various increasingly-aggravating social crises, ignore the appeal of hundreds of millions of people, and disregard the pressure from the international community. They resort to high-handed policies in dealing with the great masses. Doubtlessly, more than ever before, China has become a police state. Governments at various levels totally disregard the law and depend on violent means to solve various social conflicts. The disasters of human rights happen frequently and the rule of law has obviously suffered a retrogression.

Every day in China, there are thousands of incidents of forced demolition of houses and every year dozens of millions of people's properties are violated. As a result, there are dozens of millions of petitioners. However, the great majority of these petitioners who try to seek justice and rule of law from the higher authorities are brutally treated by the governments at various levels. Since the beginning of this year, forced demolition has caused the death of dozens of people. The citizens are violently deprived of their right of properties and other legal rights. By October, the Shanghai petitioner Feng Zhenghu has been under arbitrary detention and illegal surveillance at his residence for nearly 800 days.

The Chinese Communist government continues to severely suppress the house churches and persecute the Christians there. In April of this year, Han Hai and six other Christians from Pingdingshan City of Henan Province were sentenced from three years to seven and a half years of imprisonment by the local court on the crime of being a cult while the real reason is just because they studied the Bible on a Sunday. On June 17, 2013, Xiaodian District Court of Taiyuan in the trial of first instance sentenced Ren Lacheng, a Christian from Enyu Bookstore, to five years in prison and sentenced Li Wenxi to two years in prison on the charge of "illegal business operation."

On August 31, 2013, Liang Zhongxin, a Christian and a Sunday school teacher in a house church in Shaya County, Xinjiang, and three other people were placed under a 15-day administrative detention and were fined 1,000 yuan for giving Bible lessons to some middle school students. On July 25, 2013, a court in Inner Mongolia sentenced Christian Hu Gong to nine years in prison and sentenced Wen Weihong and Liu Aiying to eight years in prison on the same charge. According to incomplete statistics, within half a year, about a hundred house churches in over 10 provinces in China have suffered persecution. The gatherings at these house churches were raided, church properties were confiscated, religious books and other items were destroyed, believers were illegally detained and threatened, and pastors were detained.

What has aroused the most concern is the incident in which Peking University dismissed associate professor Xia Yeliang, which shows the position of the Chinese government in strictly controlling the freedom of speech. Xia Yeliang promoted China's reform towards democratic constitutionalism on the Internet. Because of this, the school came under a great pressure from the authorities and had to dismiss him. There is ample evidence that shows there is a tendency that Xi Jinping's administration is trying to control the ideology as it was done during Mao Zedong's reign.

It's sad for us to see that the status of human rights and rule of law in China is seriously disconcerting. Without human dignity or basic human rights, the modernization of China is worthless. On the contrary, when China is headed toward the opposite direction of universal values, this doubtlessly poses a greater and greater threat to America and to the civilized world. America has a proud tradition of supporting freedom and justice. In the face of the Chinese Communist government that willfully tramples on the human dignity and opposes the universal values, America should loudly show its position to the Chinese Communist government, instead of doing nothing to restrain it.

Mr. SMITH. Thank you so much, Pastor Fu. I can say that I remember when you first brought Mr. Guo's family to our attention on the subcommittee and how earnest you were that you would not cease until they were free. It has to be a source of at least some comfort, despite his horrific circumstances that he faces now, that his wife and children are safe and that attributable is to you.

STATEMENT OF MR. T. KUMAR, DIRECTOR OF INTERNATIONAL ADVOCACY, AMNESTY INTERNATIONAL

Mr. KUMAR. Thank you very much, Chairman and members of the subcommittee. Amnesty International is extremely pleased to be here to testify on this important issue.

There are two issues that we are to consider in this. First, there is an individual who has been arrested for his peaceful nonviolent political activism. And the bigger picture, U.S. policies with China, the human rights policy with China, whether it is moving in the right direction or not.

First of all, I would like to urge that my full testimony will be part of the record.

Mr. SMITH. Without objection, so ordered.

Mr. KUMAR. Thank you very much. Why is Guo Feixiong singled out and in prison? There are thousands who have been imprisoned, but in his case a couple of issues stand out. He fought against corruption. He fought for transparency. He was part of a major new citizens movement that was fighting for justice and equality in China. He was fighting for media freedom by supporting media workers, press workers, against interference in the editorial policy.

He also went to the other step of urging China to sign on to the International Covenant on Civil and Political Rights, ratify it, they have signed on, but did not ratify it yet. So we are seeing an individual here who has been fighting the fight for the needy and for justice. The results he received were that he was arrested, tortured, electric shocks were used, and he was earlier sentenced to 5 years in prison. Now he has been arrested again, again when he stood up against corruption. This time, for 2 months, for more than 2 months, no lawyers or the family members were allowed to see him. So it is basically an arbitrary detention that is taking place there.

Despite all these things, what we are seeing from our administration is the pressure that is not up to the standard that we have seen earlier. As previously, one of the Members of Congress, the Commissioner, mentioned that after Most Favored Nation was given to China the leverage for U.S. has gone. We can see that is one of the major reasons China is not worried about U.S. making statements or speaking up.

On this issue, we would like to bring to your attention an opportunity by which the U.S. can bring up the pressure in a meaningful way. As you are aware U.S. and China have two different dialogues going on. One is the annual U.S.-China Human Rights Dialogue which from our perspective, the Chinese don't take seriously. It is like a pro forma. Every year let's talk, okay, that is it. Nothing happens.

There is a serious nature of the other dialogue that takes place, that is the economic and security dialogue. The Secretary of State attends. That is when Chen was imprisoned, Secretary Clinton was there for the dialogue. That is why I meant the timing was so good that a lot of attention.

So what we are urging is that Congress should put pressure on the administration to make sure that economic and security dialogue, also include human rights. Until and otherwise, human rights become part and parcel of economic and security dialogue, whatever the U.S. says, it is not going to have any impact on Chinese.

So let us see in a practical sense to add this and some actual policy. Secretary of State will be there when human rights is being discussed. They say when we raised the issue with the administration, they say we discussed the issue on human rights during the economic and security dialogue. So why are you so hesitant to call it economic, security and human rights dialogue. So we urge strongly that Congress take this as a serious issue and exert pressure and pass resolution so that next dialogue that takes place, the dialogue is economic, security, and human rights dialogue. That is when Chinese will feel the pinch because the economy and business is tied to human rights, security is tied to human rights there. Hopefully your action, the committee's action, and other actions will bring results, to Guo Feixiong's case, but we hope that the bigger picture of having a meaningful way so that U.S. can put pressure to fight for equal justice and for human rights in China also have an impact in China.

Thank you very much for inviting us.

[The prepared statement of Mr. Kumar follows:]

Human Rights in China

Guo Feixiong and Freedom of Expression in China

Before the:

**U.S. House of Representatives
Committee on Foreign Affairs**

Testimony by:

**T. Kumar
International Advocacy Director
Amnesty International, USA**

October 29, 2013

Thank you Mr. Chairman and members of this Committee; Amnesty International USA is pleased to testify at this important hearing.

This hearing is important because of the scale of human rights abuses in China and the urgent need for the US to address those abuses.

I would first want to address the main focus of this hearing, the plight of Guo Feixiong and followed that with a review of the current human rights situation in China.

Guo Feixiong

Yang Maodong, better known by his pen-name Guo Feixiong, a human rights defender based in Guangdong province on the South China Sea coast, has been arbitrarily detained for over two months. He is at risk of torture and other ill-treatment. Amnesty International considers Guo Feixiong a prisoner of conscience, who should be immediately and unconditionally released.

Human rights defender Guo Feixiong was detained on suspicion of "gathering a crowd to disrupt order in a public place" on August 8, 2013. His sister received his detention notice on August 17. Neither his family nor his lawyer have received notification of his formal arrest, although the police have now detained him beyond the legal 37-day limit by which such a formal notice must be given. The charge of "gathering a crowd to disrupt order of a public place" carries a maximum sentence of five years in prison. He is being held at the Guangzhou City Tianhe District Detention Center, where he remains at risk of torture and other ill-treatment in detention.

Police denied Guo Feixiong's lawyers, Sui Muqing and Ling Qilei, access to him on five occasions, most recently on September 26 on the grounds that the case is of a "serious nature", and stating that the lawyers had to file a formal application to meet Guo Feixiong.

However, under China's Criminal Procedure Law, only crimes of "endangering state security, terrorism or a particularly serious crime of bribery" require lawyers to receive permission to meet with their clients.

Guo Feixiong's detention is believed to be in connection with his involvement with the "New Citizens' Movement", a grass roots movement of citizens calling for greater government transparency and an end to corruption.

In May 2012 in the article "China Needs a New Citizens' Movement", prominent human rights defender Xu Zhiyong describes the "New Citizens' Movement" as a peaceful cultural, social and political campaign. The activities he suggested people take include disseminating the "New Citizen Spirit" online and in the streets; practicing "New Citizen Responsibility" by rejecting corruption and by doing good for society; using the "Citizen" sign or other identifying methods; participating in civic life by holding meetings to discuss the political situation; helping the weak; and uniting to share and coordinate work.

Around 60 individuals have been criminally detained or subjected to enforced disappearance in the last few months in connection with this movement. Twenty-nine of these individuals are known to have been formally arrested to date.

Guo Feixiong is a writer; rights advocate and was once a legal adviser with the Beijing-based Shengzhi Law Office. He has supported various human rights causes in the past decade.

In 2005 he participated in a hunger strike in response to a call by prominent human rights lawyer Gao Zhisheng for a "hunger strike group" to protest the government's crackdown on human rights activists. The hunger strike was also a protest against his previous detention and beatings following his legal support of Taishi villagers who were calling for the ouster of a village official they had accused of corruption in 2005.

In 2007 he was sentenced to five years in prison for "illegal business dealings" (Article 225 of the China's Criminal Law). Guo Feixiong states that he was tortured into confessing this crime, leading him to attempt suicide. Guo Feixiong claims to have been deprived of sleep for seven nights, beaten and tied down for 40 days in custody in Guangzhou No. 1 detention center, Guangdong Province, in late 2006. On January 19, 2007, he was transferred to Shenyang city, Liaoning province, to "facilitate investigation." He was tortured allegedly by police who strapped him down onto a so-called "tiger bench" for four hours, hit him with an electric prod in arms and legs and genitals while hung from the ceiling by his arms and legs, and slapped him until his face was swollen. He claims he attempted suicide the following day.

In January 2013, Guo Feixiong supported the staff protest of Southern Weekly against political interference in editorial matters. In March 2013, he helped organize a signature campaign to urge the National People's Congress to ratify the International Covenant on Civil and Political Rights which China signed in 1998, but has not yet ratified.

Guo Feixiong has a wife and two children who were granted political asylum in the US in November 2009.

Current Human Rights Situation in China:

Human rights violations in China are committed on an enormous scale. Let me speak briefly to the major categories of violations.

First, hundreds of thousands of individuals are held under administrative detention, including the "re-education through labor" system. They may be detained in labor camps for up to three years without charge or trial.

Second, China often intimidates, harasses, assaults, abducts, arrests, and places under house arrest lawyers and other human rights defenders who dare to speak out against injustice or try to protect the rights of others.

Third, China continues to execute more prisoners than the rest of the world combined, usually following unfair trials with no right of appeal.

Fourth, torture by law enforcement personnel is endemic, resulting in many prisoners' deaths while in custody.

Fifth, thousands face brutal religious persecution and political repression. Religious persecution has led to the detention and repression of thousands of Tibetans, Uighurs, "unofficial church" members, and Falun Gong practitioners. Other targets of repression include democracy activists, political dissidents, advocates of political reform, and people using the Internet to disseminate information deemed by the authorities to be politically sensitive or corrosive to state authority.

Mr. Chairman, the Chinese government's record on keeping its promises on human rights has not been impressive. Assurances by authorities that the human rights situation in China would improve if Beijing were awarded the 2008 Olympics have proved false, and repeated promises to reform the system of administrative detention in China have been left unfulfilled.

Below are some of Amnesty International's specific concerns:

Freedom of Expression

The authorities continue to abuse criminal law to suppress freedom of expression. Over 100 activists, bloggers and others were criminally prosecuted, detained, or placed under surveillance following "Jasmine Revolution" inspired activities which began in February 2011, during which many sought to promote democratic reforms through street gatherings, blog commentary and other forms of activism.

Harsh criminal sentences continue to be imposed on writers, bloggers, journalists, academics, whistle-blowers and ordinary citizens for peacefully exercising their right to freedom of expression, including publishing articles or posting comments online that advocate democratic reform and human rights, exposing official corruption or malfeasance, distributing information on banned religious groups, or touching on a steadily expanding range of politically sensitive topics, including Tibet, Taiwan, and other topics which suddenly generate widespread attention online.

Administrative and Arbitrary Detention

Hundreds of thousands are arbitrarily detained in administrative forms of detention including in "re-education through labor" camps, enforced drug rehabilitation camps, compulsory psychiatric detention and "Legal Education Centers," often referred to as "brainwashing centers". They are held, often for years, without due process, including the rights to a fair and public trial by a competent, independent and impartial tribunal, access to legal counsel of one's choosing, the presumption of innocence, and the opportunity to appeal their sentence through a process of judicial review.

China also operates a growing diversity of arbitrary and illegal forms of detention. Despite having reported their closure, the authorities continue to operate hundreds of "black jails" – make-shift detention facilities used primarily to detain petitioners seeking redress for perceived injustices, for days or months. These may be located in hotels, official hostels, mental hospitals, nursing homes, and other unofficial sites.

An increasing number of human rights defenders including their family members have been put under illegal house arrest, often for years, where they may be deprived of all means to communicate with the outside world.

Forced Evictions

The forced eviction of people from their homes and farmland has become a routine occurrence in China and represents a gross violation of China's international human rights obligations on an enormous scale. Despite international scrutiny and censure of such abuses amid preparations for the Beijing Olympics in 2008, the pace of forced evictions accelerated over the past three years, as local authorities seek to offset debts by seizing and selling off land. This is in part fuelled by fiscal incentives: unlike other income streams, revenues from land lease sales are retained in full by local authorities. Such sales now account for the single largest source of revenue for local authorities. As a result, millions of people across the country have been forced from their residences without appropriate legal protection and safeguards.

Individual residents are rarely consulted about these evictions and are frequently given insufficient notice to vacate their homes. Evictees are often offered little or no compensation and inadequate alternative housing. Those who resist are routinely subjected to severe pressure and even violence. Housing rights activists and lawyers often face harassment, the loss of professional licenses, imprisonment and violence. At the same time, violence against evictees and their representatives is rarely prosecuted or punished.

Victims of forced eviction face many barriers to accessing effective remedies. Courts often refuse to accept eviction related appeals, and attempts to petition higher-level government agencies almost always fail. People who peacefully protest against forced eviction risk detention, imprisonment or detention in Re-education through Labor camps. Some resort to drastic measures, including setting themselves on fire or taking up violent forms of protest.

In January 2011, China issued regulations to outlaw the use of violence in urban evictions and granted urban owners facing evictions new protections. These regulations do not, however, provide protection to rural residents and their enforcement has been poor. Moreover, local officials continue to have a fiscal incentive to clear land for development.

Torture and Ill-treatment

Torture and other ill-treatment remains widespread during criminal investigations to extract forced confessions, and continues to be a central feature of detention for the purported goal of "re-education". Individuals detained on political grounds, in connection with exercising their right to freedom of expression, association, assembly, or belief, are often ill-treated or tortured while in custody in order to coerce them into abandoning their political or religious activities or beliefs that deemed offensive. Petitioners held in detention are routinely ill-treated and often tortured in order to coerce them into abandoning their petitioning activities. The authorities operate hundreds of "Legal Education Training Centers" across the country, designed specifically for the "transformation" of Falun Gong practitioners, where they are coerced into renouncing their beliefs. Those who refuse are at risk of escalating levels of mental and physical torture until they not only renounce their beliefs but actively cooperate with the authorities in the effort to "transform" other practitioners.

Amnesty International continues to receive reports of deaths in custody, some of them caused by torture, in a variety of state institutions, including prisons and police detention centers. Amnesty International has confirmed over a dozen deaths of Falun Gong practitioners in detention as a result of the torture associated with the "transformation" process. On June 6, 2012, veteran dissident and labor rights activist Li Wangyang was found dead in hospital just days after an interview aired in Hong Kong, in which he spoke about being tortured. The authorities claimed he committed suicide by hanging himself; however, many have questioned the likelihood of this. Li Wangyang was blind, deaf and unable to walk without assistance as a result of being tortured when he was jailed after the 1989 Tiananmen crackdown. He had been jailed twice for a total of more than 21 years.

Ethnic Minorities

The Chinese government's crackdown on any perceived challenge to its authority – which often amounts to nothing but a peaceful expression of opinion or belief – is particularly harsh against individuals belonging to minority groups including Tibetans, Uighurs and Mongolians. They continue to experience severe discrimination and to be harshly criminally punished for what authorities label "illegal religious" and "separatist" activities, but which are often peaceful expressions of cultural identity.

Chinese government policies, including those that limit use of the Uighur and Tibetan language, and severe restrictions on freedom of religion, are destroying customs and, together with employment discrimination, fuelling discontent and ethnic tensions. Such policies have led to at least 119 Tibetans to self-immolate since February 2009.

Hada, an advocate for Mongolian culture, was taken into custody in December 2010, immediately after he completed a 15-year sentence on charges of "espionage" and "separatism". His wife, Xinna, and son, Uiles, have also been taken into custody a number of times, as punishment for speaking to foreign organizations about Hada's plight.

Prisoners of Conscience

Nobel Peace Prize recipient **Liu Xiaobo** was charged with "inciting subversion of state power" and given an 11-year prison sentence on December 25, 2009 simply for co-authoring a proposal for political and legal reform in China. His wife, **Liu Xia**, has been under illegal house arrest since October 2010 and is not free to communicate with friends or the media.

Gao Zhisheng, a human rights lawyer in China, has been subjected to enforced disappearance, torture, illegal house arrest and detention as a result of his work. He has been imprisoned since December 2011 for apparently violating the conditions of his suspended three-year sentence. He has been repeatedly tortured since 2006, and continues to be at high risk of further torture.

Tibetan filmmaker **Dhondup Wangchen** was involved in making a documentary that features a series of interviews with Tibetans who voiced skepticism about the Chinese authorities' promises of greater freedom in the run-up to the 2008 Beijing Olympics. Chinese authorities suppressed the film and initially detained Dhondup Wangchen on suspicion of "illegal journalism," which is not an offense under Chinese law. He was held without charge for more than a year during which he was beaten and deprived of sleep and food. Dhondup Wangchen was tried in secret and sentenced to six years' imprisonment in December 2009. He has been tortured, subjected to solitary confinement and at times forced to work up to 18 hours a day. He suffers from various medical issues, including Hepatitis B, for which he is not receiving treatment.

US Government should urge the Chinese authorities to:

- Immediately and unconditionally release Guo Feixiong and other prisoners of conscience, who were detained solely for peacefully exercising their right to freedom of expression;
- Ensure human rights defenders can voice their grievances and exercise their rights to freedom of association, expression, assembly and movement;
- Shut down all places of detention which deprive individuals of their liberty without due process, including the rights to judicial review and safeguards against torture and other ill-treatment, and to proceed rapidly with clear and transparent plans to reform and eventually abolish all forms of punitive administrative detention;
- Thoroughly investigate all allegations of torture in custody, including those raised by alleged victims or their lawyers, provide proper redress and compensation, and end the impunity of officials who engage in torture and other ill-treatment, including by implementing the necessary institutional reforms to ensure effective enforcement of existing laws prohibiting torture;
- Immediately halt forced evictions, explicitly prohibit them by law, and ensure that adequate safeguards and protections are put in place in line with international law.

Thank you for inviting Amnesty International to testify in this hearing.

T. Kumar
International Advocacy Director
Amnesty International USA
Email: tkumar@aiusa.org

Mr. SMITH. Mr. Kumar thank you very much for that very practical incisive recommendation. I, too, have noted that human rights dialogue has almost been a cordoned-off exercise that they, the Chinese side, does not take seriously, even if the intentions on the U.S. side are very well intentioned. We are seeing the same thing replicated in Vietnam and elsewhere. It kind of puts it on the sidelines and it is not integrated with the security and economic issues so your point, I think, is extraordinarily well taken.

As far as noting that the 18th U.S.-China Human Rights Dialogue took place on July 30th through the 31st and just a few days later, Mr. Guo was arrested again. So if there was any kind of impact, it certainly was not manifested toward him as a result of the human rights dialogue. I think your point is extraordinarily well taken.

We are joined by Chairman Dana Rohrabacher. Chairman Rohrabacher, would you like to ask questions?

Mr. ROHRABACHER. Let me just make a note. I am sorry, I had three hearings at one time. I just came from a hearing on Afghanistan and if there is anything that should indicate to us that we should try to have a high standard on human rights, it's the situation we get caught in quagmires in different parts of the world. If the United States stands for human rights, and when we have individuals, brave, heroic individuals, like Guo Feixiong that what we are doing by supporting them is letting them struggle for freedom. It takes a burden off of our shoulders that we have to send our troops everywhere in the world to try to promote the cause of freedom. The fact is that by we supporting local people and their struggles for whatever tyrannical government they are under that is a way that it helps the people in the United States because then we no longer have to bear the burden of having to deal with that challenge. And with dictatorships, especially like China, a dictatorship the size of China that abuses its own people obviously has no respect for the rights of other people as well.

If China does not respect the rights of its own people to the point that it won't murder them or torture them or as we have seen with the Falun Gong where they pick them up by the thousands and throw them into prison and actually murder them for their organs, if you have a government like that or—that that is a threat to all the decent people in the world. Because if they do that to their own people, what will they do to foreigners? So we who are foreigners to them, know that here is a threat of a ghoulish group of people who are willing to commit horrendous crimes against their own people and our first line of defense is to support those of you who are struggling against that tyranny.

And Mr. Chairman, I am very honored always to sit with you, and to stand with you and the leadership you have provided on human rights issues. And especially with concern China in which as we say if China, if we can bring to a liberalization in China and support those people who are struggling, to have decent humane values in China, it will mean a great deal to the security of the United States and the rest of the world.

So thank you and I thank those of you who are struggling to help these people in China and we just want to express unity with you,

Mr. Chairman, and to these brave souls who are struggling for a better world.

Mr. SMITH. Chairman Rohrabacher, thank you so very much. I think our distinguished witnesses know that Chairman Rohrabacher, before he became a member of the House from California was a speechwriter for Ronald Reagan and was one of those who put into those speeches some of the most memorable and very enduring concepts concerning fundamental human rights and the freedom agenda so—and he has continued that ever since as an individual.

Mr. ROHRABACHER. Actually, the President was a great writer. I was just sort of helping out.

Mr. SMITH. But you wrote it too. Thank you so much. Let me ask a couple of questions and then we will go to Mr. Meadows.

Mr. Chen Guangcheng made seven very specific recommendations and observations in his testimony, of course, focusing on Mr. Guo on his fight and his deep empathy and concern which we all share.

But on one of those he talked about the importance of the Internet. And I will just note parenthetically that I have introduced and reintroduced several times legislation which is regrettably opposed by the Obama administration and that is a bill called the Global Online Freedom Act of 2013, H.R. 491, and Mr. Kumar, and Amnesty, and Reporters Without Borders, and many other organizations and NGOs have endorsed it and supported it over these many years. Part of the requirements of that legislation are to require Internet communication providers that are listed on the U.S. stock exchanges to disclose to the Securities and Exchange Commission their human rights due diligence and that means Chinese companies like Baidu and others would have to tell us what they are doing vis-à-vis human rights and if they are, as we know they are, censoring ad nauseam. That, too, would have to be disclosed.

It prohibits the export of hardware or software that could be used for surveillance, tracking, and blocking by governments of end-users in an ''Internet-restricting country,'' a new term that we invent in the bill based on a preponderance of the evidence that they are restricting the Internet and surveilling their own people. And there are other provisions as well.

Mr. Chen mentioned Hillary Clinton's statement about the Internet and allowing all members of the human race equal access to knowledge and thoughts, but this administration opposes the Global Online Freedom Act. And it would give real substance, I believe, to an effort to say we mean it when we say we want the Internet to be free, that students in China and elsewhere, but especially in China and the general public, will have access to—unfettered access to knowledge and information.

Secondly, Mr. Chen also mentioned a number of very important points, but one of them was about a Magnitsky type of piece of legislation. I think is an idea whose time has come, but we already have on the books a law that I wrote in 2000 as part of the larger piece of legislation that I was the author of called the Admiral James W. Nance and Meg Donovan Foreign Relations Authorization Act. And that is to say that anyone who is complicit in the barbaric one-child-per-couple policy and Chen Cuangcheng talks about it as being evil and wicked, which it is. It abuses women. There is no greater abuse of women's rights occurring the world and the legislation which is law on the books right now, it is not being enforced by the Obama administration and wasn't even enforced well by the Bush administration. It says that anybody who is complicit in those crimes is denied a visa to come to the United States.

We asked the Congressional Research Service to look into this last year and found that less than 30 people were penalized by visa denial and we know that there are hundreds of thousands throughout China who are visiting this unbelievable agony upon women and destroying children and young babies, especially the girl child through sex selection abortion. So that is a law that has gone unimplemented by the Obama administration.

We will redouble our efforts as we have done over and over. I asked the administration, ''What are you doing?'' ''Why aren't you implementing it?'' We get a big blank stare, but we will continue to try. But I thank you for raising the Magnitsky Act and I think as Mr. Kumar and so many others know, it does work when you hold individuals responsible for crimes in a regime that is called a dictatorship. It has a profound impact.

I wrote a law back in 2004, the Belarus Democracy Act. The mainstay of that law was to hold Lukashenka and his other fellow repressors accountable in Belarus through visa denial and well over 200 people, it's a small country, have been denied visas to come to the United States and the Europeans have followed suit. So it a model and Magnitsky is working roughly, but it is working vis-à-vis Russia today.

So I thank you for those very specific recommendations, Mr. Chen. If there are any further comments, and then I will go to Mr. Meadows, that any of our distinguished witnesses would like to make, you certainly laid out the case. We will follow this up with a letter to President Obama. We will include all of your testimony. We will ask him—he is a Nobel Peace Prize winner. He has gravitas the likes of which very few people have in the world to raise these issues and certainly now with President Xi Jinping moving aggressively in the other direction. It was already bad under his predecessor, President Hu, it has gotten worse as we all know. So there needs to be, I think, a revisiting of these issues by the administration.

And again, Ms. Yang, your comments, everyone should read, as well as your mom's, should read those comments and see a mother and daughter testifying on behalf of their husband and dad with such eloquence and such class is so moving. There is so much love coming from you toward your father and your husband. And my hope is that that will further motivate all of us who often fall asleep and don't do enough to really make a difference. Our President needs to step up. Our Congress needs to step up and we need to do much more.

And again Mr. Kumar, I love your idea of the human rights dialogues, well meaning, they don't work. We need to integrate it into the security and economic dialogues—and you are right, Secretary of State is there, and hopefully, Secretary Kerry will take these cases and take them seriously.

44

So I would like to yield to any of you and then go to Mr. Meadows for any questions he might have. If you want to comment on any of that or I will go right to Mr. Meadows.

[The following testimony was delivered through an interpreter.]

Ms. ZHANG. I have one question. On September 30th, I paid a visit to the Department of State and visited some officials there. So I made a request to the Department of State asking them to make a public announcement to ask the Chinese Government to release Guo Feixiong. But we have not seen anything that has happened. I really hope that the American Government can make an announcement.

Mr. SMITH. Could you reveal who it was that you spoke to or would you rather not do that, at Department of State?

Mr. FU. Zeya, Zeya. The Assistant Secretary, Zeya.

Mr. SMITH. Acting. Thank you. So you have reached out to the State Department and so far there has not been a response?

Ms. ZHANG. Yes.

Mr. SMITH. We will follow up as well. And I will say one statement does make for an intervention. My hope is that as we do on the Congressional-Executive Commission on China, because I am the co-chairman of that as well. We have a prisoners list. We advocate for those continuously for the release of political and religious prisoners, but we don't see a corresponding—I mean, our Ambassador Gary Locke, should be raising this. This should be a mainstay of our dialogue with China, not what is the next deal to sell more of our bombs or some other self-interest. So thank you for that. Pastor Fu.

Mr. FU. I have a quick comment about a follow up about improving the U.S.-China Human Rights Dialogue, the mechanism. Although within our human rights communities we basically concluded with the same conclusion. As Chen Guangcheng put it nicely that the human rights dialogue has become a human rights empty talk. But you know, I remembered this May when I traveled with Chen Guangcheng to the European Parliament and we met with EU's highest human rights officer, the former Foreign Minister for Greece. And he, in a private setting, but he wants our secretary to know that when Chen Guangcheng was still under house arrest and when a diplomat tried to visit, and was beaten up, right outside his Dongzhou village. And instead of making public, obviously, diplomatic protest is warranted. The EU has waited until the next round of human rights dialogue next year and talk to the Chinese Government and said, ``Why do you beat up our diplomat over there?''

So we are sort of very, very concerned on that very incident that Chinese sort of guards could beat up an EU, sort of the one of the most powerful sovereign country block could be—could keep silence for a fellow diplomat who was beaten. So after talking with Mr. Chen Guangcheng, of course, we were making suggestions to them, and I think it complied with the U.S.-China Human Rights Dialogue. One way to avoid becoming a show of empty talk is to make the human rights dialogue live streaming, to make it live broadcast. If they want to talk lies, actually the Chinese talk back to the EU and said, ``No Chen Guangcheng is free. We didn't beat up your diplomat. He is all right.''

So I think the reason the Chinese regime can pronounce these blind—just lies so unshamefully is a closed door, under the table dialogue. If it is broadcast live, even part of the session when the people around the same table, when the Chinese people and the American people and the world know what they are talking about, then it is truly—it is a true dialogue. I think you will produce some truth, some result, so that is my comment.

Mr. SMITH. Thank you very much. Mr. Meadows.

Mr. MEADOWS. Thank you, Mr. Chairman, and thank each of you for your testimony. I know it is very easy to get discouraged. The chairman has been fighting this fight for many, many years. But I can speak to his character and to his perseverance and I can tell you he is unyielding truly in his efforts to make sure that justice and fairness and compassion is something that we all revere not only here in the United States, but in China and other nations abroad. So I want to give you that encouragement.

I am a little concerned because we continue to have hearings over and over again and we ask for action items and we try to take those action items and then not much happens with them.

So Pastor Fu, let me make sure I understand you. You are saying that once we have these hearings, if we were to televise those live, that they might have some impact in terms of the human rights violations?

Mr. FU. That is right.

Mr. MEADOWS. All right. We were in a hearing just the other day where we talked about some of the media and how the truth is just not getting out, not only in China, but it is really not getting out to us as well in terms of what is happening there with regards of media personnel within China, if they report negatively. Many times their visas do not get renewed or they get delayed for long periods of time. Wouldn't you agree that that is an accurate reflection of what is happening in China?

Mr. FU. I do not necessarily agree that that happens every time or all the time. And actually, as Chairman Smith and also Congressman Frank Wolf recalled, remember before the Beijing Olympics, I remember of course they are known critics of China's human rights record and when they applied for visas, yes, they slow down a little bit, but still give you visas. Yes, you still were able to get to China, right?

I think these are peripheral concerns. I think the main concern, and as a former teacher who used to teach in the Chinese Communist Party school, I know the Communist Party's mentality is actually the weaker, or the more you yield, the weaker you show to them, actually, the more they feel they are empowered or more aggressive.

Mr. MEADOWS. So what you are saying is we need to take a more forceful hand in terms of the penalties of not complying, that we need to set laws and the State Department needs to be more forceful in terms of the potential consequences?

Mr. FU. Absolutely. It is, after all, this is two the great powers and it is not—nobody wants to have a mutual destruction.

Mr. MEADOWS. Right.

Mr. FU. But at the same time, you cannot forget our very fundamental values that form this country by just ignoring or just silencing or put human rights under the table to modernizing this very important fundamental issue.

Mr. MEADOWS. All right. Let me ask you perhaps a more difficult question. Do the Chinese people as a whole see us as being critical of human rights, being synonymous with us being critical of them as the national country or their economic—do they see those as when we are critical of human rights, being critical of them as a people?

Mr. FU. Although the Chinese Communist Party propaganda mission wants to make the Chinese regime, the Chinese Communist Party

Mr. MEADOWS. One and the same.

Mr. FU. Yes, with the Chinese people, try to mess up the idea, I think the Chinese people can make that distinction. It is really the Chinese regime who carry out this repressive policies. It is the brutal policies that is used by the torturists who tortured Mr. Guo Feixiong and Mr. Chen Guangcheng. So I think the Chinese people commit with distinction. Like even with today's hearing, with the social media and the Chinese Internet, there will be meetings with Chinese people who will know and who will even many will find the video.

Mr. MEADOWS. So what you are saying is the Chinese people would know that the Members of Congress have a warm feeling toward them. We just condemn the actions of these human rights violations?

Mr. FU. There are not only, of course, not only warm feelings, but they know that they are not fighting for freedom alone. They know you are in solidarity, their American friends——

Mr. MEADOWS. Okay.

Mr. FU [continuing]. A thousand miles away who are concerned about their prisoners, about their fellow relatives who are arbitrarily arrested.

Mr. MEADOWS. Okay. Mr. Kumar, let me go to you. Because in previous testimony and then I heard it again as a recurring theme today, you talked about the need for the State Department primarily to tie human rights and the economic viability, those together. Obviously, we haven't done a very good job of that to date. And we have had a lot of rhetoric, although I do believe the State Department has a sincere desire to affect human rights. It is a balancing act. Many times, they look at the economic impact versus human rights in trying to evaluate those two.

How do we do a better job of tying those two together in terms of—would it be to look at denying visas? How can we do that in terms of making a real impact?

Mr. KUMAR. I would anticipate that the Chinese Government take economic and security dialogue very, very seriously. It's the highest level. Secretary of State from our side, and the Foreign Minister of Chinese come together and discuss issues. They discuss economic issues and security issues together. They are tying those together.

Mr. MEADOWS. Okay.

Mr. KUMAR. But they are not tying human rights into that mix. They are having the human rights dialogue separate from that. That's why we are urging that human rights be part and parcel of this economic and security dialogue, not stand alone. When you do it stand alone, they will come, they will talk, but the pinch is not there. They are not getting the pressure. The only way they will take human rights seriously.

Mr. MEADOWS. So how do we do that? How do we take human rights and make a penalty for not complying? Because the chairman and I have been in meetings with groups from China, part of Chinese Government and their comment to the chairman and to me was, ''We are making great progress and that you are just misinformed,'' is essentially what they told Chairman Smith, that he was misinformed, that they were making great strides.

So how do we tie those two together?

Mr. KUMAR. You know, the point is if they have made any strides, of course, there are certain areas like death penalty, they have made some improvements. Earlier it was 80% of the world's executions were taking place in China. Until China changed due to lot of pressure from outside and also inside to make sure that there is another review before someone is getting executed by the Supreme Court. Because that reason, the death penalty drops to 50%, even though it is still the highest in the world. All the countries put together, it is the highest.

The issue of how to make change from U.S. in this case. The only country, by the way Congressman, that China will take seriously is the U.S. The only superpower left and they want to have good relations with the U.S. They don't want to burn bridges for something they can't do. Which is for their own interest, that's the U.S. So our suggestion is that human rights issues should be tied to these two issues, economic and security issues. Sanctioned issues are slightly different. When you—every year when they have a dialogue like with the Most Favored Nations, every year they will have to debate in Congress and at that time all kinds of human rights issues are debated. Then Congress authorizes it.

If the human rights situation goes down, Chinese fears they may not get the Most Favored Nation status renewed. That's, you know, the liberty that was dropped, actually under the Clinton administration that was dropped.

So the other alternative we are seeing is there is another dialogue taking place even though there is no sanction related, the mere fact the highest levels of U.S. administration in the foreign ministry, that's the Secretary of State. In this case, Secretary Kerry will be there raising the issues, not a human rights bureau or another human rights bureau. There is one good example we have to see. Qing's case, Qing who testified. Secretary Clinton was there for the economic and security dialogue, so when the whole issue blew up there and, you know, your hearings, Mr. Chairman, I also testified when he was making his appearance by phone from his hospital bed, that put pressure on Secretary Clinton to have some decision. And in turn they exert pressure and we have seen him released.

So what it shows is if the pressures goes in a meaningful way in the highest levels that it will have some impact.

Mr. MEADOWS. So you are saying that at the Secretary level or the Under Secretary level and just make sure that they are at those high levels?

Mr. KUMAR. High level, but the way you tie is you tie human rights with economic and security dialogue. That's when they will take it seriously. That's me saying we raised it, the administration is reluctant, they know the Chinese will not like it.

Mr. MEADOWS. Mr. Chairman, if you will indulge me for one more question, if that would be all right? I assume that it is.

One of the understandings that I have is when we have events, whether it be arrests or whether it be rebellion, whether it be a protest, that social media and everything lights up, it flickers up. And then at that particular time that there is, you know, just an oppressive—on the Internet freedom it gets—really, there has to be a desire to jump the firewalls, so to speak, to allow that message to continue to get out.

We heard the other day, or I heard in a briefing the other day, that once we jump the firewall that many times they are subject to cyberattacks, almost instantaneously at the same time. Again, to suppress the freedom of the press or the freedom of speech from sharing that.

Would you agree that that is a significant problem, and if we could address that with additional server capacity would that help the Chinese people share the story? Either one of you, Pastor Fu or?

Mr. FU. Yes, I think the public meeting and also a statement mentioning specific names, I think that will really demonstrate to leadership, you know, like the case of Chen Guangcheng, like the Guo Feixiong. You know, I remember months ago with Jared Genser, the president of Freedom Now, who actually yesterday had an op-ed in The Washington Post. We together met with President Obama's top human rights officer near the White House, and basically our key demand our or key point is President Obama, you know, he can just basically use his presidential leverage to tell— or even privately communicate with the Chinese, even face-saving matters, say, look, this is a concern, not only to me but to the American people, you know, the torture, the arbitrary arrests, you know, with Guo Feixiong and the Nobel Peace winner, Liu Xiaobo, and of course, Mr. Guo Feixiong. I mean, all these cases, and their family members are here. They are at the door of the White House and if you don't release them I will meet with them.

And in fact, the Speaker of the House, John Boehner, and the Minority Leader, Nancy Pelosi, twice already, I know for a fact, that along with several committee chairmen, including Chairman Smith, wrote letters to President Obama, asking him to meet with Guo's wife, asking him to meet with Chen Guangcheng. And so far not even a Cabinet-level member has ever even met with the family members. I think the Chinese are watching. The Chinese, of course, are observing whether that is the priority within the administration.

Mr. MEADOWS. Perhaps we can call on the President's compassion for people and encourage that even today. But I thank you.

Mr. Chairman, I yield back. I appreciate your indulgence.

Mr. SMITH. Mr. Meadows, thank you. Yes, Mr. Fu?

Mr. FU. I just want to correct on record, I think I got to know the Acting Assistant Secretary, Ms. Zeya. She did mention Yang Maodung's name last week at China's U.N. UPR review in Geneva.

So that is the only name mentioned by any other country. Of course, the Chinese Ambassador rejected that immediately. So I wanted to keep that record straight.

Mr. SMITH. Thank you. I think we do have votes—yes, Ms. Zhang?

[The following testimony was delivered through an interpreter.]

Ms. ZHANG. I am very thankful to Chairman Smith. You gave us this opportunity on my husband, Guo Feixiong's behalf. I hope that this hearing can produce some positive result to help my husband. And I hope that Congress and the administration can work together for the earlier release of my husband.

Mr. SMITH. Ms. Zhang, thank you so much. Again, your bravery and that of your daughter just mirrors that of your husband and it's an inspiration to all of us.

You know, we begin every single session of Congress with a prayer. I think it would be most fitting, especially now since the cruelty in China has escalated, and it has already been bad for so long and many of you have suffered from it, Pastor Fu, but it would be very appropriate if Pastor Fu, if you could just lead us in a very brief prayer for the freedom of this wonderful husband and father, Guo Feixiong, and others who are suffering the barbarity of this regime in Beijing. If you could just lead us in that, and that will be the close of this hearing.

Mr. FU. Dear heavenly father, we thank you for this wonderful opportunity to testify for the truth about freedom, about democracy, about all these brave spirits, that we know that every human being is created with your image which gives us the true source of dignity and equality and justice. So as we are created equal, we can seek justice and justice for all. Lord, we thank you for this great country, a country that has been founded by the Founding Fathers with this great Constitution, with the guarantee of freedom of religion, freedom of assembly, freedom of speech. Lord, we cannot take this for granted, because, as your servant, Martin Luther King said, "Injustice anywhere is the threat to justice everywhere." Lord, may you lead us to be a voice for the voiceless, because in the end those victims, those who are silenced, will remember not the words of enemies, but the silence of their friends. Lord, may you use this panel, use the Members of Congress, use the leadership of the great United States of America and use the leadership of President Obama and Secretary of State John Kerry to be a vehicle to not only advance the business, trade interests of America, but more importantly advance the freedom, democracy, and the human dignity, the value of these universal imperatives throughout the world. At the end of the day, we do not live by food and water and worldly entertainment only, but more importantly, we live to glorify you and to love our neighbor and to love each other. May you grant freedom for Guo Feixiong sooner. May you grant freedom of Gao Zhisheng sooner. May you grant freedom of many others sooner using us. We pray all this in Jesus' name. Amen.

Mr. SMITH. The hearing is adjourned.

[Whereupon, at 4:31 p.m., the subcommittee was adjourned.]

A P P E N D I X

Material Submitted for the Hearing Record

SUBCOMMITTEE HEARING NOTICE
COMMITTEE ON FOREIGN AFFAIRS
U.S. HOUSE OF REPRESENTATIVES
WASHINGTON, DC 20515-6128

Subcommittee on Africa, Global Health, Global Human Rights, and International Organizations
Christopher H. Smith (R-NJ), Chairman

October 29, 2013

TO: MEMBERS OF THE COMMITTEE ON FOREIGN AFFAIRS

You are respectfully requested to attend an OPEN hearing of the Committee on Foreign Affairs, to be held by the Subcommittee on Africa, Global Health, Global Human Rights, and International Organizations in Room 2255 of the Rayburn House Office Building (and available live on the Committee website at www.foreignaffairs.house.gov):

DATE: Tuesday, October 29, 2013

TIME: 2:30 p.m.

SUBJECT: Guo Feixiong and Freedom of Expression in China

WITNESSES: Ms. Zhang Qing
                            Wife of Guo Feixiong

                            Ms. Yang Tianjiao
                            Daughter of Guo Feixiong

                            Pastor Bob Fu
                            Founder and President
                            ChinaAid Association

                            Mr. Chen Guangcheng
                            Chinese human rights activist
                            (*Appearing via videoconference*)

                            Mr. T. Kumar
                            Director of International Advocacy
                            Amnesty International

By Direction of the Chairman

The Committee on Foreign Affairs seeks to make its facilities accessible to persons with disabilities. If you are in need of special accommodations, please call 202/225-5021 at least four business days in advance of the event, whenever practicable. Questions with regard to special accommodations in general (including availability of Committee materials in alternative formats and assistive listening devices) may be directed to the Committee.

COMMITTEE ON FOREIGN AFFAIRS

MINUTES OF SUBCOMMITTEE ON *Africa, Global Health, Global Human Rights, and International Organizations* HEARING

Day___*Tuesday*___Date___*October 29, 2013*___Room *2255 Rayburn HOB*

Starting Time ___*2:31 p.m.*___ Ending Time ___*4:32 p.m.*___

Recesses |___*0*___| (___to___) (___to___) (___to___) (___to___) (___to___) (___to___)

Presiding Member(s)

Rep. Chris Smith

Check all of the following that apply:

Open Session ☑   Electronically Recorded (taped) ☑
Executive (closed) Session ☐   Stenographic Record ☑
Televised ☑

TITLE OF HEARING:

Guo Feixiong and Freedom of Expression in China

SUBCOMMITTEE MEMBERS PRESENT:

Rep. Steve Stockman, Rep. Mark Meadows

NON-SUBCOMMITTEE MEMBERS PRESENT: *(Mark with an * if they are not members of full committee.)*

Rep. Robert Pittenger*, Rep. Dana Rohrabacher

HEARING WITNESSES: Same as meeting notice attached? Yes ☑ No ☐
(If "no", please list below and include title, agency, department, or organization.)

STATEMENTS FOR THE RECORD: *(List any statements submitted for the record.)*

TIME SCHEDULED TO RECONVENE_____
or
TIME ADJOURNED ___*4:32 p.m.*___

Subcommittee Staff Director

www.ingramcontent.com/pod-product-compliance
Lightning Source LLC
Chambersburg PA
CBHW080445290526
45791CB00008BA/2610